Kicking
ASS
in a Corset

Kicking ASS in a Corset

JANE AUSTEN'S 6 PRINCIPLES FOR LIVING AND LEADING FROM THE INSIDE OUT

Andrea Kayne

UNIVERSITY OF IOWA PRESS | IOWA CITY

University of Iowa Press, Iowa City 52242
Copyright © 2021 by the University of Iowa Press
www.uipress.uiowa.edu

Printed in the United States of America
Design by April Leidig

Printed on acid-free paper

Library of Congress Cataloging-in-Publication Data
Names: Kayne, Andrea, 1966– author.
Title: Kicking Ass in a Corset: Jane Austen's 6 Principles for Living
and Leading from the Inside Out / by Andrea Kayne.
Description: Iowa City: University of Iowa Press, [2021] |
Includes bibliographical references and index.
Identifiers: LCCN 2021000458 (print) | LCCN 2021000459 (ebook) |
ISBN 9781609387600 (paperback; alk. paper) | ISBN 9781609387617 (ebook)
Subjects: LCSH: Leadership in women. | Self-esteem in women. |
Austen, Jane, 1775–1817—Characters.
Classification: LCC HQ1233.K39 2021 (print) | LCC HQ1233 (ebook) |
DDC 155.3/3382—dc23
LC record available at https://lccn.loc.gov/2021000458
LC ebook record available at https://lccn.loc.gov/2021000459

For my mother,
Margery Charron Kayne,
who led me to the well within

Contents

Acknowledgments

Striving to be internally referenced does not mean you don't need people to help you realize your vision. Certainly, many people have helped me achieve mine.

Maureen Collins, my dear lifelong friend and Janeite soul sister, was there when this work was conceived and added so much Jane Austen perception, wit, and brilliance to each draft. The director of University of Iowa Press, James McCoy, channeling Elizabeth and Darcy, provided frank, insightful, and intelligent feedback that made this a much better book. I also want to thank Allison Means, Rebecca Marsh, Susan Hill Newton, and all of the other amazing people at the University of Iowa Press who put their talent, care, and hard work into this book.

Editor and literary midwife Katy Sprinkel Morreau furnished invaluable assistance every step of the way. My research assistant (and stepdaughter), Ruby Mead, provided wonderful help distilling the stories of kickass leaders and becoming a master of the Jane Austen "pink books" and the *Chicago Manual of Style*. Donna Kiel, the director of DePaul's Office of Innovative Professional Learning, has been instrumental in operationalizing this work and fleshing out the exercises, helping to establish professional development courses and a coaching program based on this work. I deeply appreciate my colleagues at DePaul who have been generously supportive of my work, especially Dean Paul Zionts and my chair, Sonia Soltero. I could not have put this work into the world without the amazing creativity and other-worldly competence of Jessie Jury, who makes all things possible. I'm grateful to Jane Wesman for believing in me and the book and so ably spreading its message.

Many internally referenced Austenesque women (and men) have inspired me and this work with their stories of wisdom, courage, hope, and transcendence in one form or another. These include, but are not limited to, Jeannie Aschkenasy, Heidi Bailey, June Brought, Sharon Chuter, Linda F., Christine Blasey Ford, Carol Henriques, Susan Hyman, Paul Julian, Ellen K., Sandy Lerner, Kimberly Lloyd, Lori Lovens, Abby M., Kathleen Medina, Jacque Nelson, Renee P., Jennifer Farrell-Rottman, Vicky Tsai, Sr. Frances Ryan, Jian Sun, Greta Thunberg, Marcy W., Cookie Weber, Keith Westman, and Cassie Zheng.

I am so very grateful that my dear soul sister Kathy Bresler and her ALTAR empowerment community have been such a vital force in bringing internally referenced leadership to me and the world.

Thank you to my dear friends Terri and Greg Reisig, who took a joyous pilgrimage to the Royal Crescent and to Chawton House with me in search of Jane's spirit, and now, Greg's spirit, too.

Finally, I must thank the most important beings in the world to me. My wonderful son, Josh, who teaches me about compassion, care, and curiosity, and what it means to be a truly loving human. My amazing daughter, Ariel, who teaches me about values, voice, and vocation, and what it means to be an authentic and powerful woman. My husband, Andy Mead, who teaches me that the sun, music, and *Persuasion*-style second-chance love come from the same divine place. And my Pride and Prejudoodle, Addy, who is as golden as they come.

Kicking
ASS
in a Corset

INTRODUCTION

What Would Jane Do?

"I am only resolved to act in that manner, which will, in
my own opinion, constitute my happiness, without reference
to *you*, or to any person so wholly unconnected with me."
—Jane Austen, *Pride and Prejudice*

What can organizational leaders in business, education, government, and most any enterprise learn from an unemployed, unmarried woman who lived in patriarchal, misogynistic rural England more than two hundred years ago? As it turns out, a great deal. I've witnessed this firsthand as a professor and director of the graduate leadership program in the College of Education at DePaul University. My professional life as a leadership expert has coincided with my lifelong interest (some might say obsession) with Jane Austen's heroines and, specifically, with their internal fortitude, steadfast strength, and quiet command in the face of extremely confining and sometimes oppressive circumstances.

For more than twenty years, I have taught countless aspiring school principals and superintendents and educational leaders in higher education about using their limited resources to navigate the challenge of education law, the restriction of the politics of education, and the often-fraught relationships among educational stakeholders. As a leadership consultant I have worked with many education, government, corporate, and technology leaders and organizations to assist them in maximizing their efficacy, improving their efficiency, and enhancing their impact in spite of limiting constraints, diminishing resources, and overwhelmed systems. For the female graduate students and consulting clients I work with, there is often an added layer of constraint to overcome. The ubiquity of gender discrimination, gender inequity, and a sense of gendered powerlessness have created additional obstacles and burdens for women occupying or seeking leadership positions.

In the course of my work, I point to well-known role models in education, business, and government to illustrate the characteristics of internally referenced leadership and to show how particular women leaders have successfully navigated difficult work and gender dynamics. Surprisingly, however, it is the comparison not to modern-day examples but to Jane Austen's heroines that makes the most impact on the participants I'm addressing—regardless of whether they've read Jane Austen. My take on the Jane Austen role models has been presented to great effect at several national conferences, including the Women in Educational Leadership Conference at the University of Nebraska and the Jane Austen Society of North America General Meeting.

Jane Austen's heroines are inspiring and useful because they provide a way of finding one's power and agency under great constraint and in trying times. The "corset" is an apt metaphor to describe the constrictions female leaders in many industries and organizations are facing these days. Women in the workplace may find it difficult to "breathe" as they are pushed, prodded, and squeezed by seemingly intractable forces beyond their control. The ubiquitous pressures on women leaders and aspiring leaders include insufficient credibility, disrespect, pressure to be likable, absence of mentors and sponsors, lack of confidence, inadequate visibility, office politics, limited negotiating experience, gender discrimination, financial inequity, gendered career paths, disproportionate family responsibility, limited access to networks, linguistic style, sexual harassment, and so much more. These external aggravating forces make it particularly challenging to succeed as a leader, to survive as a leader, or to get promoted to leadership in the first place.

This dynamic of constraint has only been exacerbated in the age of Trumpism and the fear-based leadership culture that it represents. Whether it is Democrat representative Alexandria Ocasio-Cortez, who in response to vicious sexist remarks, boldly exclaimed, "I am someone's daughter too," or Republican representative Lynn Cheney, who was chauvinistically undermined for merely doing her job in questioning government policy, congresswomen on both sides of the aisle and other women leaders in United States government experience the stifling effects of gender bias. Anne Kaiser knows this. One of the most powerful members of the Maryland state legislature and chair of its Ways and Means Committee, Kaiser explains, "Ask any woman leader out there: The fact is that some men simply resent women leaders, and truthfully, so do some women."[1]

More than ten years ago, I was unexpectedly too prescient for my own liking and published an article about this fear-based leadership in the *Journal of Women in Educational Leadership* titled "You're Fired! Donald Trump, No Child Left Behind, and the Limits of Dissonant Leadership in Education."[2] Using research and theory based on emotionally intelligent primal leadership, I discussed the destructive consequences of dissonant, fear-based leadership, policy, and practice. In the years since that article was published, my experience has further shown me that those conscious, emotionally intelligent leaders, who are what I conceptualize as internally referenced, end up thriving in any environment, no matter how constricting or how dissonant.

Although my theory of internally referenced leadership relates to other leadership theories, such as Emotionally Intelligent Primal Leadership, Conscious Leadership, and Authentic Leadership, it is distinct and different in its focus. The internally referenced leader is emotionally intelligent, conscious, and authentic, and she also strives to achieve an overarching sense of personal agency and self-reliance in any and all external environments, no matter how challenging or even how advantageous. An unwavering internal locus of control directs her perceptions and actions and is always what is most important. This is what distinguishes internally referenced leadership from other leadership theories that focus more on dealing with external realities than maintaining an internal and unwavering state of well-being and equanimity despite what is going on. While some theories do address the importance of those internal states, they do not provide specific and integrated operationalized guidance for achieving them.

These principles of internally referenced leadership work together to help create leaders and organizations who truly operate from the inside out in order to withstand the pressure and vagaries of difficult external circumstances. Similar to the ice skater, mountain climber, or surfer who prepares for the demands of her sport by learning Pilates to strengthen her core, the internally referenced leader develops practices for strengthening the metaphoric core that enables individuals and organizations to remain steady, sturdy, and strong, no matter how precarious the environment. The tools and practices of internally referenced leadership help us become leaders in our own lives, living on our terms, in spite of the pressure we feel to conform or capitulate.

This is the only leadership theory whose principles and guidelines have been inspired by the writings of an uneducated, unmarried female fiction writer from the 1800s. Along with my graduate students, consulting clients, and colleagues, those who have attended my speaking engagements and workshops appreciate the distillation, applicability, and relevance of these unexpectedly modern and relevant instructions for internally referenced leadership from Jane Austen, an unlikely and untraditional leadership expert. Austen's characters provide a framework for success that is as revolutionary now as it was two centuries ago.

When I taught these principles to a group of female Chicago police officers, they were struck by the realization that they were constrained by many kinds of "corsets" but their male counterparts were not. The fifty educators in Beijing I worked with even connected these principles to aspects of the *Tao Te Ching* regarding the illusory nature of seeking external power. A group of women who were going through divorce found that these principles helped them find some sense of power and agency even amidst life-altering situations that seemed beyond their control. A group of young women in tech used these principles to initiate a dialogue with their manager addressing power dynamics in their workplace. Indeed, the six principles for internally referenced leadership inspired by Jane Austen have impacted women in many different circumstances. No matter who they are, they have been inspired, uplifted, and empowered by Elizabeth, Elinor, Anne, Fanny, Catherine, and Emma.

Each of these heroines represents an aspect of internally referenced leadership by sourcing her power from within even while living in confining circumstances. Through their various strategies, these fictional women from the 1800s achieve a kind of independence and personal agency that is astonishing and unexpected in patriarchal Regency England and is even revelatory today.

Jane Austen's six principles for internally referenced leadership are as follows:

1. Like Elizabeth Bennet from *Pride and Prejudice*, know your own internal and inherent value, especially in external environments that intentionally or unintentionally devalue you or create other outer conditions of unworthiness.

2. Like Elinor Dashwood from *Sense and Sensibility*, respond to external tumult and adverse change with an internal calm, acceptance, and problem-solving resilience rather than as the passive victim of external circumstance and self-pity.

3. Like Anne Elliot from *Persuasion*, choose, create, and claim paradigms based on internal worthiness, hard work, and merit over external constructs that bestow the shortcuts of privilege, entitlement, and membership in the "right" club.

4. Like Fanny Price of *Mansfield Park*, insist on faithfully following your internal moral compass and normative principles, even in the face of external pressure, coercion, and material consequence.

5. Like Catherine Morland of *Northanger Abbey*, protect and retain your internal childlike dreaming, wonder, curiosity, passion, and hope—especially in an external world that can be discouraging, disillusioning, and filled with despair.

6. Like Emma Woodhouse from *Emma*, constantly be willing to learn from an internal place of openness and humility rather than from a stance of perfection and superiority.

In *Jane Austen's Women*, author Kathleen Anderson says,

Jane Austen's novels are not fantasies; their female protagonists must square off with adversity and face down the reality of disappointment, deferral, dearth, and death, but still accept responsibility for their own emotions and actions. Regardless of the plot twists out of their control, they must exercise and strengthen their hearts, minds, and spirits. As part of this endeavor, Austen insists, they can create their own happiness, or they should at least try.[3]

This is internally referenced leadership in a nutshell. No matter what happens to a leader or aspiring leader—even when she has very little power and very few resources in a patriarchal world—she can exercise strength and control of heart, mind, and spirit and ultimately find her own peace and equilibrium. Whether things are going well or not so well, she is not plugging into the outside world for happiness or satisfaction.

Anderson observes that Austen "presents as a distinctly female problem the question of how to cope with limited control over one's quotidian life" and "targets women with her message of self-determined mental stability."[4] She continues, "Austen acknowledges but does not grant women the excuse of gender injustice or other adversities as absolution from seeking emotional as well as physical and marital self-determination."[5] Jane Austen's heroines offer surprisingly practical instructions for female leaders to be self-determined even when they perceive they have little control. As Holly Luetkenhaus and Zoe Weinstein have noted,

> Austen's texts especially are primed for the resistance that fandom is known for because they were resistant themselves. Aja Romano notes that "fandom is subversive. If a canonical worldview is entirely straight-white-male, then fans will actively resist it." Austen's novels are telling women's stories within the straight-white-male society in which she lived, so Austen fandom is an ideal space to continue to explore women, nonbinary people, and others who have felt that their experiences and voices are ignored by mainstream media.[6]

Reading Jane Austen through the lens of internally referenced leadership has been a wake-up call for me. She encourages women to claim their power from the inside out. The world needs female leaders, and it needs a new female paradigm of leadership for everyone. Take, for example, New Zealand prime minister Jacinda Ardern. As Tina Brown said of Ardern's comprehensive and distinctly female response to the Christchurch mosque shootings,

It's past time for women to stop trying to cram themselves into outdated NASA spacesuits designed for an alien masculine physique. Salvation doesn't lie in pursuing traditional male paths of ejaculatory self-elevation. In drawing on women's wisdom without apology and pushing that wisdom forward into positions of power, we can soothe our world and, maybe, even save it.[7]

Again and again I have seen this two-hundred-year-old six-point formula for internally referenced leadership work not only for devoted Janeites but for all kinds of people in all kinds of situations. This book unpacks each principle by examining it in the context of Jane Austen's original text, Jane Austen scholarship, and literature on leadership and management. The chapters illustrate how each principle relates to and further develops the theory of internally referenced leadership, illuminated with real-life examples and strategies gleaned from the pages of Austen's work.

Austen has been a lighthouse for me, both personally and professionally, during those many times I have felt as if I'm flailing in the dark at the behest of external forces beyond my control. While she reminds us that "[w]e none of us expect to be in smooth water all our days,"[8] she offers a way home—home to ourselves. This book attempts to articulate the need for and the way to internally referenced leadership by drawing our attention to Austen's insights about our internal sources of power. We need Jane Austen now more than ever: we need her strategies about transcending her misogynistic environment so that we can transcend our own.

"Universal Truths" Are Anything But

Like Elizabeth Bennet from *Pride and Prejudice*, know your own internal and inherent value, especially in external environments that intentionally or unintentionally devalue you or create other outer conditions of unworthiness.

Meet Elizabeth Bennet

Pride and Prejudice begins with the iconic first line, "It is a truth universally acknowledged, that a single man in possession of a good fortune, must be in want of a wife."[1] For Jane Austen and her beloved heroine Elizabeth Bennet, this statement is very much an irony. *Pride and Prejudice* is the story of clever, irreverent, and independently minded Elizabeth, who lives in the English countryside with her parents and four sisters. When a wealthy eligible bachelor, Mr. Bingley, moves into their neighborhood, Mrs. Bennet, Elizabeth's high-strung, overbearing mother, becomes obsessed with his marrying one of her daughters.

This does make some sense given the limited opportunities for young women in the 1800s and the meager dowries of the Bennet daughters, whose portions are "unhappily" small.[2] To add to their financial insecurity, the family home is entailed and will be inherited not by any of the daughters but by their distant cousin, the odious Mr. Collins. Mrs. Bennet's marriage plan seems to be going well. Mr. Bingley is very interested in Jane, Elizabeth's warm and beautiful sister, who also has feelings for him. Mr. Bingley's oldest friend, the proud and snobbish Mr. Darcy, however, undermines their burgeoning relationship even as he himself finds himself falling for the combative and irreverent Elizabeth. Elizabeth does not subscribe to the universal truths of her community and refuses to be with someone she doesn't like or respect, declaring that he is "the last man"[3] whom she would ever marry. At the end of the book, when Mr. Darcy is about to approach Elizabeth again for marriage, his aristocratic aunt, Lady Catherine de Bourgh, confronts Elizabeth and asks her to promise not to become engaged to her nephew. In defiance, Elizabeth makes it clear that she will not promise anything, declaring that she is living "without reference" to Lady Catherine "or to any person so wholly unconnected"[4] to herself. The novel explores what it takes for Elizabeth to come together with Darcy, while still being true to herself.

A Truth Universally Acknowledged

"Well-fixed universal truths" are anything but. As an internally referenced leader, you identify your own "truths" as distinguished from the socially constructed "truths" of others.

I admit it; I felt like a fraud. For years, I had been trying to get on the board of trustees of the prestigious private school where my children attended at the time. I was finally there, but I continually wondered whether I truly belonged. Most of the other board members were white men from the world of business—finance, real estate, corporate law—while I was from the field of education. Looking back, it is strange that I would somehow think my education experience wasn't as valuable or relevant. After all, as far as I knew, I was one of the few board members who had studied the theory of progressive education associated with the school's namesake, Colonel Francis Parker, and his colleague John Dewey while at the Harvard Graduate School of Education. I understood the school's whole-child mission and student-centered educational leadership decisions in ways many of my colleagues did not; and yet, perplexingly, I still felt as though I did not bring as much value to the board as they did. This erroneous thinking and what I experienced as disproportionate power from the leaders of the board resulted in what scholars call Muted Group Theory,[5] a situation where I felt marginalized and silenced by the dominant discourse of the group.

My conflict about my voice (or lack thereof) on the board came to a head when it was time to elect new officers. While Parker prided itself on being progressive and diverse in many areas of school life (which it was), the slate of new officers (as usual) consisted entirely of white businessmen. Two of them even worked at the same financial services company. When I came on the board, I was told that most of the board work happened in committee and that the executive committee, which was comprised of the officers and chairs of the various committees, held the most power of all. The rest of the board was expected to follow whatever the executive committee recommended. We were told to vote for the slate of officers presented because the executive committee thought we needed "strong businessmen" for an upcoming capital campaign and building expansion. This seemed pretextual to me; Parker was always in the midst of a capital campaign and building expansion in some form or another. But I did not dare say anything as I felt obligated to follow the board norm, rubberstamping whatever the executive committee wanted. I was expecting to vote yes, and I was *expected* to vote yes. I was expected to be a good girl: obedient and quiet.

It was hard to be a good girl, however, when I looked over and saw another girl in the room—my then–sixteen-year-old daughter, Ariel. Ariel served as a student representative and ex officio member of the board. On a recent road trip to visit Washington University in St. Louis, we had listened to Sheryl Sandberg's *Lean In* and Taylor Swift's *1989*, and now she was looking at me with a glare that seemed to be asking, *Why aren't you shaking it off and leaning in*? I wanted to explain that it was a universal truth that I didn't belong on this board and had to do what the executive committee said and that, according to the establishment status quo, white male businessmen were more valuable than I. But were these truths really mine? My daughter looked at me with the smart, sharp, skeptical, no-BS eyes of Elizabeth Bennet.

In response to Ariel's unspoken challenge, I took a deep breath, took out my pen, and scrawled a personal values mission statement on the back of the meeting agenda. "I value gender, racial, ethnic, SES, and discipline diversity in all aspects of organizational leadership so that the organization can realize its vision, purpose, and serve as many stakeholders as possible. I also value modeling moral courage for my children." Wherever possible, an internally referenced leader acts in accordance with her values mission statement. Looking at my daughter, I raised my hand and objected to the lack of diversity in the slate. My protest gave permission for the few other women and people of color who were on the board to also express their concerns about the lack of representation. The officers withdrew the slate and presented a more diverse offering at the next meeting. The board and school ultimately benefited from a more inclusive board; and they even invited me to run for secretary the following year, citing the impact of my educational experience and voice for marginalized points of view. The ending of this anecdote, however, does not feel satisfying, for I doubt I would have ever spoken my truth had Ariel not been in the room.

An internally referenced leader knows and speaks her truth and is skeptical about the existence of what other people call universal truths or even what we ourselves have accepted as universal truths. From the very first line in *Pride and Prejudice*—"It is a truth universally acknowledged, that a single man in possession of a good fortune, must be in want of a wife"—Jane Austen suggests that most of what we consider universal truths are merely socially constructed values "well fixed" in the minds of those around us.[6]

Pat Rogers, editor of the Cambridge edition of Jane Austen's *Pride and Prejudice*, tells us that this most famous first line "parodies the use of generalised assertions at the start of moralistic essays."[7] It has also been explained that Elizabeth's ironic wit allows her to "disown" the "most disreputable truths" of her "overbearing society."[8] Thus, Jane Austen dares us and empowers us to disregard seemingly entrenched social norms and values by turning them on their heads—by questioning them, laughing at them, and ultimately, if they do not comport with our own values, rejecting them. This is what the most authentic and effective internally referenced leaders do.

The most effective leaders are able to question the values of those around them and reject those values when appropriate. They can do this because they know their own values going in; they know what they stand for first—before confronting any situation or any external judgment. Babson College business professor Mary C. Gentile launched the *Giving Voice to Values* curriculum as a collaboration between the Yale School of Management and the Aspen Institute. It addresses the importance of defining one's personal and professional purpose "explicitly and broadly before values conflicts arise."[9] We need to strive to understand what we care about and what is important to us irrespective of any person or situation. We must define ourselves on our own terms separate from any other condition. Critical to becoming an effective and authentic leader is self-awareness of our internal values as the basis for intrinsic motivation. It is crucial for leaders to reflect on what matters to them and why it matters. When the seventy-five members of the Stanford Graduate School of Business Advisory Council were asked about the "most important capacity for leaders to develop," they were nearly unanimous in responding that it was "self-awareness" of who we are and what is important to us.[10]

Emotional intelligence gurus Daniel Goleman, Richard Boyatzis, and Annie McKee maintain that emotionally self-aware leaders know who they are because they are attuned to and driven by their core principles, which emanate from the inside out. Specifically, they explain that

> leaders high in emotional self-awareness are attuned to their inner signals, recognizing how their feelings affect them and their job performance. They are attuned to their guiding values and can often intuit the best course of action, seeing the big picture in a complex situation. Emotionally self-aware leaders can be candid and authentic, able to speak openly about their emotions or with conviction about their guiding vision.[11]

The internally referenced leader is aware of who she is and what she believes independently of any specific external influence or context. She is true and in touch with her unwavering authentic self, which is consistent between her personal and professional lives. She strives to always be herself and, like Elizabeth Bennet, refuses to be subjugated or subordinated in order to fit into someone else's value structure.

Elizabeth Bennet, Jane Austen's much-beloved and irrepressible heroine of *Pride and Prejudice*, is unquestionably more self-aware and consistently herself than many real people I know.

Perhaps she is an ideal to which we aspire even if we have material responsibilities that she did not. Elizabeth knows her own value and worth at all times and in all situations. She knows who she is and what she stands for and does not deviate from her guiding principles and truths in good times or in bad times or then again in good times, as we follow the pendulum swing of the plot through the course of the novel. She easily rejects many of the social norms and values of her society, preferring instead her own independent assessment of what the world is and should be. She even has the audacity to value herself in ways that society does not value her.

De-Universalizing Our Truths

Through Elizabeth, Jane Austen teaches us that to be internally referenced leaders, we must de-universalize our truths. We need to understand that those things we think of as *fixed* or *settled* or *sacred* or *just the way it is* are not necessarily so. Uncover those subconscious forces and factors—family, community, organizations, employers, celebrities, and other influencers—that we have allowed to trespass on our thinking, to invade our minds and beliefs about our world and ourselves without our even realizing it.

Alicia Menendez warns about the subconscious "shoulds" in *The Likeability Trap*. She explains that because many women want to be likable "good girls" in the workplace, they internalize other peoples' opinions into directives about how to think and what to do. Moreover, they have probably been doing this their whole lives. Following these external voices at the expense of our authentic voices can create resentment, dissatisfaction, and feelings of alienation at work and at home. As Menendez writes, "the process of disentangling all these expectations and learned behaviors" that comprise our "shoulds" is complex but can be done.[12]

According to Mary Gentile, "if we define our professional

purpose explicitly and broadly before values conflicts arise, it becomes easier to normalize" them in our lives.[13] The process, inspired by Elizabeth Bennet, that I have used for myself, my students, and my clients to de-universalize our truths and normalize our authentic values involves giving thought to whether the principles and values under which I am acting are really mine. The first step is to take inventory of dissonant emotions and the underlying trespass on personal values that they might reveal. The emotions that arose for me at that board meeting evoked many conflicting claims: *I am lucky to be on the board because I don't really belong and I shouldn't jeopardize my place by shaking things up*; *I and others have diverse expertise and diverse voices that could add a lot of dimension and insight to our executive committee discussions, deliberations, and actions*; *if I speak my truth, everyone will hate and exclude me*; *standing up for my truth is much more important than being liked*; *my role is to be loyal, supportive, and obedient to those in power no matter what*; and *I want to show my daughter that it is much more important to be her authentic self than to shapeshift so that others will like her*.

The next step in de-universalizing our truths is to ask whether the values that prompted the dissonance come from our authentic self or from the voices of people in our lives whose disproportionate influence we have internalized. The obedient good girl "shoulds" were not my truths. My tumultuous childhood included well-intentioned but limited fear-based adults who communicated explicitly and implicitly that, as a young girl, I was not worth as much as others and therefore had to earn my place through unwavering obedience, sacrifice, and diminishment of self. Internalizing these values from my childhood messaging has served a purpose in my life. It's been a strategy that enabled me to successfully navigate and be a dutiful soldier in home life, academic life, employment life, . . . or so I thought. What I have learned from Jane Austen is that the fearful protection from other people—the paranoid mentoring—in the end requires that we turn on ourselves.

Even with all the work I have done, this ubiquitous "be a good girl" recording can make itself heard when I am in a faculty meeting, presenting at a consulting workshop, or meeting with a client. If I don't identify these so-called universal truths as not my authentic truths, they can undermine the way I speak (or don't speak) at work and at home. As women and girls, many of us were socialized to forgo our own values and truths for those of others. We were told to be quiet, to be small, and to be like everyone else except ourselves. In a *Harvard Business Review* anthology about women and leadership, noted Georgetown linguistics professor Deborah Tannen explains that the ways girls are raised can lead to women in the workplace who subordinate themselves. They spend too much time acting modest, apologizing, avoiding verbal opposition, and being indirect.[14] Elizabeth Bennet is a reminder to go back to the original factory settings, before we were socialized to be small. Even though, as the odious Mr. Collins noted, Elizabeth Bennet's "portion" was "unhappily so small,"[15] she never apologized nor was indirect when it came to living her own values and knowing her own worthiness.

A Portion Unhappily So Small

A portion "unhappily so small" is true only if you believe it. As an internally referenced leader, you strive to value yourself inherently and unconditionally from the inside out.

Marcy worked at one of the most successful family law firms in Los Angeles. We met at a women's leadership conference, where she offered to buy me coffee if I'd be willing to hear about her "well paid but stifling corset"—the law firm where she worked.

She was having trouble fitting in at the office. Unlike her partners, whose application of family law was "extended scorched-earth litigation," with all the fees it brought in, she preferred the relatively more peaceful, expeditious route of mediation. She explained that compared to her law partners, she was a lot more concerned with the impact of divorce on everyone in the family unit, especially the children and even the spouse on the other side.

Marcy knew the importance of this from her own experience. Her parents went through a particularly brutal divorce with lasting repercussions. To this day, she never wanted to host Christmas at her home because her parents still weren't speaking, even after twenty-two years, and she refused to pick sides. Marcy resented that as a child she was placed in the middle of her parents' toxic power struggle. She described in vivid detail what it was like to be fourteen, throwing up in the bathroom the morning she "was forced to testify against" her father in a child support hearing. As an attorney, she tried to do everything she could to make sure everyone got through divorce in a way that was as "healing and whole as possible."

Marcy, herself, however, did not feel whole. She knew her clients appreciated her skill, but she told me "she would not be satisfied" until the partners at her law firm "validated her approach and her worth." She wanted me to help her convince her law partners of her value to the firm. When I refused to begin our work together by creating a spreadsheet to document her value to the organization, Marcy was disappointed.

Inspired by the internally referenced leadership of Elizabeth Bennet, however, I felt my first (and maybe only) job was to convince Marcy of her value to herself. We went over the criteria her partners used to define success, which included billable hours, length of lawsuit, and an assessment of "how badly the other side was beat." We talked about whether this reflected what was important to her. Marcy explored how her own criteria differed from the criteria of her partners, and together we developed a custom rubric to determine success on her terms. Her criteria included things such as how quickly the case settled; how peaceful the process was; and how well the children and parents were doing as the divorce was finalized and how they were doing one year later. When she used her personal rubric of success, Marcy had to acknowledge that she was indeed thriving. Moreover, once Marcy learned to define success for herself, she ended up actually bringing more money to the firm as word of mouth spread and women, in particular, sought her out to represent them because of her healing approach to an inherently stressful process.

An internally referenced leader knows her own inherent worth and is skeptical about any external valuation of her just as Elizabeth Bennet was dubious about external valuation of her. In Jane Austen's time, there was no better way to place a societal value on a woman than to speculate on her prospects in the marriage market. For an unmarried woman such as Elizabeth, with hardly any dowry, the likelihood of a good match or even a decent one was very dim indeed. Elizabeth Bennet, however, values something more important than marriage and materialism. This shocks everyone around her, especially the first two eligible gentlemen whose marriage proposals she rejects.

The first rejection is to her father's cousin and heir to Longbourn, her family's estate: William Collins. Mr. Collins is also an eligible match as the clergyman at Hunsford Parsonage near Rosings Park, the great estate of his patroness, Lady Catherine de Bourgh. Given Elizabeth's unfortunate financial circumstances, Mr. Collins is dumbfounded and cannot believe her rejection of his marriage proposal. As David M. Shapard comments, "being motivated only by such material considerations himself, Mr. Collins undoubtedly finds it hard to imagine anyone else being spurred by different motives. . . . Now that he has been thwarted, Mr. Collins begins to reveal the crassness beneath his extravagantly polite exterior."[16]

He is utterly shocked at her rejection and replies with disbelief, saying, "You must give me leave to flatter myself, my dear cousin, that your refusal of my addresses are merely words of course."[17] Given Mr. Collins's eligibility from a societal perspective, he cannot believe Elizabeth would refuse his proposal. He is insulting and demeaning as he points out her lack of value in society's eyes:

> It does not appear to me that my hand is unworthy [of] your acceptance. . . . My situation in life, my connections with the family of De Bourgh, and my relationship to your own, are circumstances highly in my favour; and you should take it into farther consideration that in spite of your manifold attractions, it is by no means certain that another offer of marriage may ever be made you. Your portion is unhappily so small.[18]

Patricia Meyer Spacks suggests that Jane Austen's satire of Mr. Collins and his "nasty" reply describing Elizabeth's lack of value on the marriage market reflects Jane Austen's rejection of society's definition of value.[19] Similarly, Ivor Morris describes Mr. Collins as "the living expression and microcosm of all those things against which [Austen's] soul is in revolt."[20] While Collins represents value based on superficial externalities such as status, money, and aristocratic associations, Elizabeth values others and herself based on intrinsic qualities such as integrity, intelligence, and wit. She does not substitute other people's notions of value and worthiness for her own.

As Kathleen Anderson observes,

> What is Jane Austen's ultimate vision of the "accomplished woman"? On the one hand, her heroines of integrity reject marriage-market motives as the basis of self-cultivation, and she undercuts

the assumption that women's worth depends on extrinsically measurable qualities. Elizabeth Bennet boldly defies nearly all the standards for female excellence cited by Caroline Bingley.[21]

Award-winning journalist and talk show host Mika Brzezinski wrote an entire book about how women in the workplace outsource their value. In *Know Your Value* Brzezinski interviews business and financial expert Suze Orman, who points out that "a woman is socialized to accept that which she is given. So if somebody tells you that you can't, you believe it. If somebody says you're not worth it, you believe it. You get angry, but you can't say anything because women don't say what they think and they don't do what they feel."[22]

Elizabeth Bennet goes against the grain; she is a woman who says what she thinks and what she feels regardless of the consequences. Internally referenced leaders do not compromise their values or their valuing of themselves for anyone, even when they are stuck in confining situations; they are emotionally free because they value themselves irrespective of how society or their workplace values them.

Separating Ourselves from Our Portion

Elizabeth Bennet exemplifies how an internally referenced leader does not value herself based on her occupation, her material possessions, or her connections. She exemplifies nonattachment in that she does not define herself by her portion or others by theirs—even if other people do. In this way, she can maintain a strong state of internal well-being and homeostasis when things are going poorly or even when things are going well. She anchors within so that her self-worth does not follow the dowry, the stock price, the gross receipts, the number of Twitter followers, the colleges her children attend, or any other external marker used to compare and elevate. Success can be as dangerous as so-called failure if we outsource power to any external data point. When our well-being is dependent on something outside ourselves, we live with a low-level agitation, knowing that the external marker may change at any time. That is why it is so important to follow Elizabeth Bennet's lead, contradicting Mr. Collins and separating ourselves from our portion, however great or small.

It can be very difficult, however, for women in particular to separate themselves from their portions, especially as they relate to other people. Many of us are relational and are accustomed to defining ourselves in terms of metrics in comparison to other people or by what we do for other people or in conformance to what other people think of us. While a woman's tendency toward social connection can be helpful, desirable, and even laudable, a focus on that alone can undermine her sense of self—for who are we in the absence of anyone else? In her seminal work, *In a Different Voice*, Carol Gilligan describes how women's need to identify themselves through their relationships or service to other people can lead to "dissociation from themselves."[23]

Preoccupation with others can also lead to dissociation and separation in the workplace. Relegating women exclusively to the relational realm of caring for others can disadvantage them at work, compared to their male counterparts, especially as they seek leadership roles. Research has shown that women employees tend to be perceived as "Taking Care"[24] while male employees are often perceived as "Taking Charge." The "Taking Care" behaviors perceived as more feminine include (1) supporting, by "encouraging, assisting, and providing resources" for others; (2) mentoring, by "facilitating skill development and career advancement" of others; (3) networking, by "developing and maintaining relationships" with others; and (4) team-building, by "encouraging positive identification"[25] with others in the organization.

While these are important skills and attributes in the business environment, they are not as highly valued as the more stereotypical male "Taking Charge" leadership attributes. Women can, however, take care and take charge. In fact, women leaders have been praised for both during responses to global crises like the COVID-19 pandemic. Bethany Garner writes that, according to Rosabeth Moss Kanter, professor of business administration at Harvard Business School, "empathy and decisiveness are the two key traits that have allowed female leaders to succeed through the coronavirus crisis. Empathy allows these leaders to quickly grasp the severity of the situation, while timely decision-making means action is taken quickly."[26]

It can be very difficult for women to see themselves beyond their roles as caretakers, whether at work or home. In working with women leadership groups, I often notice the tendency for the participants to define themselves relationally as caring for others. For example, I asked participants in a female mastermind group I was facilitating to name their most meaningful strengths. Almost every person responded by describing the role they played in someone else's life: *I'm a supportive team leader; I'm a caring mother; I'm an inspiring mentor; I'm the glue that holds our department together; I'm a spouse who helps my partner be their best self;* and *I rally the troops at work and at home when times are difficult.*

When I passed out a second index card and asked the group to name a meaningful strength that did not involve service to another, they took much longer to write. Eventually the group came up with internally referenced strengths, having nothing to do with other people and not necessarily confined to their roles at home and work. These included attributes such as these: *Creativity flows whenever I tap into that inner well; I laugh from my belly and can see twisted humor in almost everything; I may be 5′ 4″ but I can walk down the street like I'm nine feet tall;* and *I sleep well most nights, knowing I tried hard.* It can be very difficult for us to define ourselves irrespective of other people, but it is absolutely crucial for internally referenced leadership and for an internal sense of power that stabilizes us. An internally referenced leader tries to remember her internal well-being and state of equanimity no matter what other people think, say, or do. She tries to see herself on her own terms, beyond what Henri Nouwen describes as the "three lies of identity," which are "I am what I have; I am what I do; I am what other people say or think of me."[27]

In Elizabeth Bennet, Jane Austen has created a character who, uncharacteristically for women in the 1800s and even today, is described on her own terms, having nothing to do with her subservience as daughter and potential wife. She is portrayed by phrases such as "uncommonly intelligent" with a "lively" and "playful" disposition that resulted in her "delighting in any thing ridiculous."[28] Whether before she meets Mr. Darcy or when she rejects him after his first marriage proposal or even when she accepts his second marriage proposal and marries him to join one of the wealthiest families in England, her strengths remain unchanged. Throughout the entire course of the novel (and her fictional life), we are told that she is still lively, witty, playful Lizzy Bennet. At the very end of the novel, Jane Austen explains that Elizabeth and Darcy "were able to love each other, even as well as they intended . . . though [Darcy's sister Georgiana] often listened with an astonishment bordering on alarm, at [Elizabeth's] lively, sportive manner of talking to her brother."[29] Elizabeth does not use her improved externalities to change how she feels about herself.

Thus, Elizabeth's value remains constant no matter how her external environment changes for the worse or better and no matter with whom she interacts. She represents the capacity to utilize an internal locus of control in order to have agency over how we perceive ourselves or our surroundings—no matter how our society views us. She both challenges us and empowers us to define our own norms and values proactively instead of waiting to be defined by someone else's. Finally, she encourages us to remain steady in our self-definition and self-regard inherently and unconditionally.

The "Last Man in the World" Test

Rejecting "the last man in the world" requires completing your own circuit. As an internally referenced leader, you source your power from within before, during, and after any external condition.

June Brought, a leadership collaborator of mine, works in corporate wellness for the successful women's clothing company Eileen Fisher. The company has flourished since its founding in 1984, currently earning revenue of more than $300 million a year. What truly sets the company apart, however, is its early adoption of conscious capitalism and a sincere desire to enhance the lives of all its stakeholders. Eileen Fisher was one of the first clothing companies that insisted on using sustainable materials such as organic cotton, and implemented programs to reduce fabric and fiber waste. Eileen Fisher's philanthropic efforts focus on business leadership grants to develop and benefit the careers of young women around the world. The company is also committed to enhancing the well-being of its own employees at every level, which is why June was hired.

According to June, "Eileen Fisher is not just another company that claims to care about the well-being of its employees but really only cares about how they can contribute to the well-being of the bottom line. Eileen Fisher truly is concerned with its staff as human beings first." One of the tools June uses to help individuals at Eileen Fisher and elsewhere find a healthy balance between life and work involves what she calls "completing your own circuit." She believes it is essential that we plug into our own beings first in order to feel empowered, fulfilled, and complete. As June explains, when we outsource our power to a job, a romantic relationship, or any external condition, "we compromise our emotional welfare and risk having someone cut off our power." She says that completing our own circuit involves a deep internal knowing that "we are fully charged and complete unto ourselves without any need for outside support or validation."[30]

Admittedly a fictive metaphor, Elizabeth Bennet's initial rejection of the powerful Mr. Darcy is an instructive parable of completing one's own circuit. While on the face of it Mr. Collins seems like a respectable match, he definitely lacks integrity, intelligence, and especially wit. Thus, Elizabeth's companions (with the exception of Charlotte Lucas) might excuse her rejection of him based on the fact that he is a pompous, obsequious idiot. Elizabeth's associates, however, would be absolutely shocked and horrified at her rejection of Fitzwilliam Darcy's first proposal. After all, Mr. Darcy is the most eligible bachelor in all of Regency England: not only intelligent, tall, and handsome, he is owner of the great estate of Pemberley, with an income of more than £10,000 per year.

With even less sensitivity than Mr. Collins, however, Mr. Darcy's first proposal contains insults and condescension, as he very directly (and cruelly) points out Elizabeth Bennet's lack of value on the marriage market and the dishonor she and her family would bring to him and his family. Although he is telling her he loves her and wants to marry her, his language and tone are demeaning and condescending; and when she points this out, he expresses no contrition.

Under the guise of frankness, he seems to relish his arrogant behavior. Darcy boasts, "Nor am I ashamed of the feelings I related. They were natural and just. Could you expect me to rejoice in the inferiority of your connections? To congratulate myself on the hope of relations, whose condition in life is so decidedly beneath my own?"[31] This cruel outburst is probably due in part to his shock at her rejection. Given their disproportionate value in society's eyes, it is difficult to understand why anyone and especially Elizabeth with her meager dowry would reject him even given the insulting nature of his proposal. David M. Shapard surmises,

> It is remarkable that a man as intelligent as Darcy would speak so insultingly. One cause is undoubtedly his strong feeling of pride, along with the frankness (which he boasts of shortly) that makes him hesitate to disguise these feelings. Another factor is his evident confidence in being accepted, which keeps him from worrying too much about antagonizing Elizabeth. Finally, it is possible that, in his myopic way, he conceives of his words as a compliment—as if to say, "Even though I object to your family and social position, your personal charms are so great that I am overlooking all that"—and expects her to receive them as such.[32]

In response to his insults of her, Elizabeth Bennet makes it abundantly clear that the societal view of Mr. Darcy's proposal is not necessarily and never was "natural and just" to her. With a confidence that is unwavering, she replies,

> From the very beginning, from the first moment I may almost say, of my acquaintance with you, your manners impressing me with the fullest belief of your arrogance, your conceit, and your selfish disdain of the feelings of others, were such as to form that ground-work of disapprobation, on which succeeding events have built so immoveable a dislike; and I had not known you a month before I felt that you were the last man in the world whom I could ever be prevailed on to marry.[33]

Spacks explains, Elizabeth's response to Darcy reveals that her "forthright rejection of Darcy issues not only from her 'prejudice' against him but from her personal integrity."[34] Kathleen

Anderson notes that in rejecting Darcy, "Elizabeth asserts her right of self-determination."[35] It was not just her fictional protégées to whom Jane Austen recommended not compromising one's values and feelings in marriage. In 1814, Jane Austen writes a letter to her niece Fanny Knight encouraging her to break off a relationship:

> And now, my dear Fanny, having written so much on one side of the question, I shall turn round & entreat you not to commit yourself farther, & not to think of accepting him unless you really do like him. Anything is to be preferred or endured rather than marrying without Affection; and if his deficiencies of Manner &c strike you more than all his good qualities, if you continue to think strongly of them, give him up at once.[36]

Negotiating guru William Ury might describe Elizabeth Bennet's ability to walk away from one of the richest men in England as reflective of a kickass inner BATNA. BATNA stands for "best alternative to a negotiated agreement." Ury is the coauthor of the classic 1981 text *Getting to Yes: Negotiating Agreement without Giving In*;[37] he more recently wrote what he calls "the missing first half" of his classic tome, which is entitled *Getting to Yes with Yourself: (And Other Worthy Opponents).*[38]

The basic thesis of this important work is that we need to come to terms with ourselves before we can come to terms with anyone else. As an example similar to completing one's own circuit, Elizabeth illustrates how to live in full knowledge of her inner BATNA. In other words, like Elizabeth Bennet, we need to feel our own power from within before and during any interaction with the outside world. Ury (2015) writes,

> We can, however, increase our power from within in a way that is always available to us, no matter what our outer situations might be. In a negotiation or conflict, well before we develop

an *external* alternative to a negotiated agreement, we can create an *internal* alternative to a negotiated agreement. We can make a strong unconditional commitment to ourselves to take care of our deepest needs, *no matter what* other people do or don't do. That commitment is our inner BATNA. Genuine power starts inside of us.[39]

Elizabeth Bennet's inner BATNA is so strong that she asserts her genuine power independent of any person or condition. In order to assess whether or not we are an internally referenced leader who is closing our own circuit, Jane Austen might recommend what I call "The Last Man in the World" Test.

For me, Elizabeth's saying *no* to Mr. Darcy's first proposal is one of the most important and empowering passages I have ever read. It can be applied to the fields of leadership, psychology, and feminist studies. Even though she has no money and no prospects, she firmly says, "I felt that you were the last man in the world whom I could ever be prevailed on to marry."[40] She is okay and complete within herself. This gives her extraordinary power to be able to walk away from a potential material savior. Jane Austen suggests that Elizabeth Bennet is not for sale no matter how dire her situation.

I know it is unrealistic to assume that women in the workforce can just walk out of their jobs and snub their employers the way Elizabeth shuns Darcy. This is very difficult to do when there are mortgages, student loans, and the need for health insurance. Career expert and coauthor of *Fire Your Boss* Stephen Pollan, however, asserts that even without leaving a specific workplace, we can complete our own circuit by radically changing our attitudes *about* our jobs and employers. He calls this new perspective an "inside job" and explains that "it's done by adopting an entirely new attitude toward work and the workplace, one that puts you in charge of your job. The trick is to 'fire your boss' and replace him or her yourself."[41] Finding an empowering inner BATNA while stuck in a constraining employment situation can enable you to think beyond your current job and feel more powerful even when waiting for the right opportunity to make a move.

A self-taught graphic designer and single mother, Abby admired Elizabeth Bennet's courage to stand up to Mr. Darcy but could not imagine any way she could afford to stand up to her employer. "Elizabeth Bennet may not have had a dowry," Abby told me, "but she also didn't have to provide health insurance and college tuition for her kids." Abby had worked for a small marketing firm, running their design department. She liked her boss "as a fellow human" but felt that he "did not recognize her creativity, leadership, and insights." Moreover, while she didn't think it was intentional, she observed that men were treated with more respect than women and were "valued more as equal professionals."[42]

She truly felt stuck. She was worried that if she stood up to her employer, he would take it personally and there would be subtle (perhaps unconscious) retaliation. This is a valid fear for many women. In a *Harvard Business Review* publication entitled *The Memo Every Woman Keeps in Her Desk*, USC Business School scholar Kathleen Reardon warns that "we still have a long way to go" and that even in light of the #MeToo movement, a woman's decision to speak up may be very risky: there is no guarantee "a male CEO will listen and appreciate such unsolicited input."[43] Abby feared that if she left her job, she would not be able to get another position of equal stature given that she was primarily self-taught and didn't have the education and formal training that many graphic designers and especially graphic design managers have.

In order to "free" herself of her employment situation without confronting or leaving, Abby had to think about herself as a professional beyond this current job. What skills did she have? Were there aspects of her portfolio that she wanted to enhance? There was no reason she couldn't work on these and think beyond her job even while she was still working at her current position. The mere idea of exploring resources for expanding her repertoire made Abby feel excited and creative in ways that she hadn't in a long time. Researching online graphic design degree and certificate programs, in particular, gave her a sense of agency. She was taking steps to empower herself to get a new position even if she wasn't ready to look for one yet.

Abby ended up enrolling in an online certificate program in graphic design at Parsons Design School in New York. While she has not left her original job yet, she is enjoying the stimulation of her program, impressing her professors with the advanced knowledge she brings to the classes, and collaborating with some students on freelance work. She is enhancing her inner world so that she can create options in the outer world, but she isn't waiting for the external opportunity in order to feel powerful and free.

Without Reference to You or Any Person Wholly Unconnected

Acting "without reference to you or anyone wholly unconnected" involves putting yourself at the center of your life. As an internally referenced leader, you live in self-referral as opposed to object-referral.

As women leaders and women in general, it is so easy to value and define ourselves with respect to our connection to others and by what we do for others. We are someone's daughter, someone's wife, someone's mother, someone's sister, someone's caregiver, and the list goes on. The same thing happens at our places of work. We define and value ourselves based on whether we please our employers, our employees, our clients, our constituents, our shareholders, and the list goes on. This gender differentiation exists in society and in our workplaces. Researchers have found that women leaders tend to be valued for being "collaborative and communal" and when they are not, they are chastised for being "bossy or aggressive."[44] As women, we are often conditioned and expected at home and work to serve and please those around us.

Even though her society demands it of women, Elizabeth Bennet does not live to serve and please the patriarchal world in which she lives. Her inner stability in knowing her own worthiness, principles, and values precludes her from sourcing power outside. Similarly, the most conscious leaders source their power internally rather than externally. According to *The 15 Commitments of Conscious Leadership*, the most effective leaders source their approval, control, and security from inside rather than living from the belief that "approval, control, and security come from the outside—from people, circumstances, and conditions."[45] Jim Dethmer and his colleagues note that one of the key differences between a conscious leader and an unconscious leader is whether she sources her power from within or without. As Dethmer (2015) and his colleagues explain,

> all leaders at any moment are operating from one of two beliefs/
> experiences: those who believe they lack something and want
> it and are seeking to get it from someone or something outside
> of themselves, and those who believe they are already whole,
> perfect, and complete and lack nothing. Those leaders move in
> the world from a very different energy. Those who believe they
> lack move in the world from fear and those who believe they are
> already whole, perfect, and complete, lacking nothing, move in
> the world from love and creativity.[46]

Elizabeth Bennet can reject both Mr. Darcy's devaluing of her and society's devaluing of her because she values herself first, before anyone else. Thus, she references approval, control, and security internally despite what is going on in her environment.

Internally referenced leadership challenges us to define ourselves irrespective of our connection to what we do for other people. While Jane Austen wrote two hundred years ago, well before the existence of the Conscious Leadership movement, her most beloved heroine, Elizabeth Bennet, epitomizes an enlightened leader distinguished by the fact that above all else, she completes herself.

Elizabeth's inner BATNA is on full display as she confidently sets a very firm boundary to the aristocratic and powerful Lady Catherine de Bourgh. Lady Catherine heard rumors that Mr. Darcy, her nephew, was going to propose to Elizabeth for a second time. She calls Elizabeth an "obstinate, headstrong girl!"[47] She presses Elizabeth for confirmation or denial of the engagement; she lambasts her and her family and bemoans the disgrace the marriage would bring to Mr. Darcy. Elizabeth refuses to confirm or deny the rumors by emphatically asserting her internally referenced regard of herself, independent of any societal view or external criteria:

> You have widely mistaken my character, if you think I can be worked on by such persuasions as these. How far your nephew might approve of your interference in his affairs, I cannot tell; but you have certainly no right to concern yourself in mine. . . .
>
> . . . I am only resolved to act in that manner, which will, in my own opinion, constitute my happiness, without reference to *you*, or to any person so wholly unconnected with me.
>
> . . . And with regard to the resentment of his family, or the indignation of the world, . . . it would not give me one moment's concern.[48]

Anderson notes that in this scene, "Elizabeth Bennet claims her right to subjectivity and to fulfillment for her own sake."[49] It reflects what the author of the widely acclaimed *The Making of Jane Austen*, Devoney Looser, calls "the image of a witty

Elizabeth thwarting the wishes and imperatives of the traditional and the powerful, in favor of her own desires and will. In these scenes, Darcy seems almost beside the point, a fortunate afterthought, a just dessert for Elizabeth's cleverness, self-assertion, and confidence."[50]

Elizabeth's internally referenced confidence epitomizes what Deepak Chopra calls "self-referral." In *The Seven Spiritual Laws of Success*, Chopra distinguishes between "self-referral" and "object-referral." In a state of self-referral, our internal reference point is our own spirit and not the objects of our experience. This is in contrast to a state of object-referral, in which we are influenced by objects outside the self, including situation, circumstances, people, and things. Leaders in a state of object-referral are ineffectual because their thinking and behavior are always in anticipation of a response and in need of approval and, therefore, are fear-based.[51]

In self-referral, the internally referenced leader is whole before, during, and after any external circumstance, whether positive or negative. Even toward the end of the novel, when Mr. Darcy evolves and reveals his generous spirit, and develops humility so that Elizabeth accepts his second proposal, Elizabeth does not essentially change. She goes from being a likely old maid with little money to someone who is marrying one of the wealthiest, most important men in England, and she still is as witty and smart and internally referenced as she was before. She is engaged, both literally and figuratively, without being attached because she always sources her self-regard from within.

Cutting Cords with the Wholly Unconnected

It is such a powerful moment when Elizabeth Bennet kicks Lady Catherine de Bourgh off her property and tells her she will act "without reference to [Lady Catherine], or to any person so wholly unconnected" with her.[52] The phrase "wholly unconnected" reminds the internally referenced leader to cut cords with those external forces and people and situations that tie her down.

We need to ask about the forces that keep us small and hold us back—the ones that make us feel stuck. In many ways, the external conditions we desperately seek to escape are already wholly unconnected, and it is just our misperception that makes us feel we are enmeshed and tethered. We also need to be just as careful about those external situations that make us feel too self-important, especially when we use them to prop ourselves up. If we plug into success for our well-being, we may constantly be fearful of losing it. We can maintain a sense of peace only if it is sourced from inside.

Elizabeth Bennet exemplifies the internally referenced leader who consciously chooses not to define herself by her external achievements even when things go well. It can be easy and tempting to rely on measures such as stock price, movie grosses, school district test scores, poll numbers, and Facebook "likes" to inform us of our worth. These external data points are shallow and ephemeral and will never fill us up. Like Elizabeth Bennet, an internally referenced leader holds her success lightly, grounded in her own independent worthiness. Elizabeth would agree with the *Tao Te Ching* adage, "Success can be as dangerous as failure."[53]

Marrying Our Own Selves with a Capital *S*

Elizabeth Bennet does end up marrying Mr. Darcy at the end of the book. By the time of his second proposal, he has been chastened, and she has also learned about the goodness of his character, which had been there the whole time. (Perhaps he taps into his internally referenced leadership.) And it is a happy ending. But I would argue that Elizabeth's marriage to Mr. Darcy is not nearly as important as her marriage to her real and authentic Self (with a capital *S*, rather than the generic self with a lower-case *s* that society ascribes to her). She knows who she is, she knows what she values, and she is her best marriage partner. Totally comfortable with herself, she won't change that Self for anyone or anything. She won't compromise her values; and her own valuing of herself has nothing to do with whether she is married to Mr. Darcy or not or whether she lives at Longbourn or Pemberley or rents a small room in Lambton. Before, during, or after any opportunity or challenge, she is with herself fully. As internally referenced leaders, we commit to our own values and valuing of ourselves.

How to Put Elizabeth in Your Life

We put Elizabeth in our lives when we strive truly to live from the inside out. We do this by examining and, where relevant, purging those so-called universal truths and *should*s that we have unconsciously picked up along the way that don't reflect who we really are or what we really want. Living inspired by Elizabeth requires completing our own circuit so that we source our power from within before, during, and after any external condition. We put ourselves at the center of own lives so that we live in self-referral as opposed to object-referral. Finally, we know we are channeling Elizabeth when we value ourselves with steadfast constancy, irrespective of anything we achieve or don't achieve in the outside world.

Exercises for Operationalizing Principle 1

➤————→

1. Create a Truth Inventory and Shuck the "Shoulds."

Write down a list of your ten most important "truths" that reflect your values.

Put your list away for a day. Now honestly examine each truth and decide whether it is yours or whether you obtained it as a "should" from someone in your external environment (your parents, your boss, your spouse, your friend group). Ask yourself whether the truth or value from your outside world reflects what you believe now and comports with who you are on the deepest level. Write each truth that is not your own on a small piece of paper and shred it, claiming that Elizabeth Bennet mantra, "My courage always rises with every attempt to intimidate me."[1] Create a new list of the truths that are truly your own.

2. Create a Personalized Rubric.

A rubric is a set of criteria that can be used for self-evaluation. What specific criteria are important to you to define success? How will you list those criteria in your personalized rubric? How does your rubric differ from the external rubric of success of those around you (your parents, your boss, your spouse, your friend group)? Why are your criteria important to you, and how can you keep them foremost in your mind?

3. Explore the Other Side of Your Business Card.

On the other side of your business or index card, write down three words that express your value that have nothing to do with your work or what you do for others. Recite them aloud regularly, reminding yourself of your inherent value and worth.

4. Cutting Cords with the Wholly Unconnected.

Which people, situations, and paradigms in your life do you perceive to be holding you back? Visualize yourself cutting the cords to this extra weight you don't need that is holding you back. Finally, an optional step as you cut the cord is to say—out loud or to yourself—with Elizabeth Bennet confidence, "It is time for you to go. I am resolved to act in a manner that will constitute my happiness without reference to you or to any person so wholly unconnected with me."

2

Being "Mistress of Myself" Ain't Easy, Sister

Like Elinor Dashwood from *Sense and Sensibility*,
respond to external tumult and adverse change with an
internal calm, acceptance, and problem-solving resilience
rather than as the passive victim of external
circumstance and self-pity.

>———➤

Meet Elinor Dashwood

Elinor Dashwood is introduced as "the eldest daughter, whose advice was so effectual"[1] that she "possessed a strength of understanding, and coolness of judgment, which qualified her, though only nineteen, to be the counsellor of her mother."[2] Indeed, Elinor takes charge of reviving her family after her father dies. His passing dramatically alters their lives as primogeniture laws require him to leave his estate to John, the eldest son from his first marriage. While Mr. Dashwood on his deathbed extracts a promise from John to financially care for his stepmother and stepsisters, John's greedy wife, Fanny, and his own limited character result in his giving them nothing.

Elinor's mother and sister Marianne have difficulty facing their destitute situation. Elinor, who has "a better acquaintance with the world"[3] as it is, accepts their circumstances and mobilizes them. Virtually penniless, they take the charity of a cousin who offers them a small cottage on his property in Devonshire.

The sisters navigate their new life in contrasting ways; Marianne leads with intense emotion, while Elinor's "feelings were strong; but she knew how to govern them."[4] Marianne falls in love, very passionately and publicly, with the handsome and duplicitous John Willoughby. He suggests that he will propose to Marianne but suddenly disappears without any explanation. Again, Marianne experiences profound devastation, with violent emotion on full public display.

Elinor also experiences heartbreak but keeps it to herself, promising not to disclose that her romantic interest, Edward, was unavailable due to a prior, ill-conceived engagement. When Marianne finds out about Elinor's silent months-long suffering, she chastises herself for her lack of regard for Elinor's well-being. "So calm!—so cheerful!—how have you been supported?"[5] she asks. Elinor explains that her sense of "duty" and "exertion of spirits"[6] got her through her loss of Edward and the loss of their father. Elinor also relies on this strength when Marianne suffers a life-threatening illness.

After Marianne recovers, she settles on a sober, calm, and stable romantic attachment with Colonel Brandon, a family friend who has been in love with her since they moved to Devonshire. Unexpectedly, it is rational Elinor who experiences an intense, passionate love as she and Edward are reunited when he is released from his prior engagement. As Edward approaches her at the end of the novel to propose, Elinor's eyes well up, and she says to herself, "I *will* be calm; I *will* be mistress of myself."[7]

A Better Acquaintance with the World As It Is

As an internally referenced leader, you accept difficult realities instead of avoiding, denying, and pushing against them. Ellen told me that the fall of 2014 "was a crazy time," which she remembers "as if in a fog and zombie-like state," though she tried to be as effective and efficient as she could. "But," she admitted, "it was hard getting things done when I didn't know where I was half the time." She describes a day when she was particularly out of it—a day when her judgment was obviously flawed since she had made a Genius Bar (tech support) appointment at the Apple Store on Black Friday. The store was packed as she waited for the service rep to assist her with her laptop issues. To pass the long wait, she scrolled through the massive numbers of emails on her phone. She recalled her experience this way:

> I was so behind in my response time to people. . . . I had been in triage mode, only focusing on what absolutely needed my attention. But there were so many people who I had been ignoring and who had no idea what had been going on in my life. One of the many people I had been ignoring was Linda, so I felt incredibly guilty and mortified when I ran into her also waiting at the Genius Bar.

Ellen and Linda worked together on a leadership council for women executives, and Linda chaired a committee on which Ellen also served. Ellen hadn't attended the September and October meetings and didn't explain why she hadn't responded to Linda's emails. Ellen said she had been "overwhelmed and quite frankly didn't know what to say." But Ellen confessed that she felt bad about it. Linda had always been nice to her, so she felt she deserved the truth, even if in a very loud, buzzing Apple Store.

"I'm so sorry I didn't attend the meetings or respond to your emails," Ellen explained. "You see, I unexpectedly separated from my husband, and I've been focusing on the change in our family, my kids, my work, and figuring out the next steps and how we move forward, and trying to get through the holidays. The holidays are tough."

Ellen told me that she didn't want to go into any more detail:

I made it a point to try not to tell other people—and especially myself—stories about judgment or blame. There was just no room for that. If our marriage had been a branch that died long ago and needed to break off from the tree, why would I blame the storm for serving its final blow? As unexpected and harsh as the storm was, perhaps it was doing us all a favor in the long run?[8]

She wouldn't tell me any more, only that her situation was "very complex and multifaceted and beyond any one cause or person."

It was, therefore, strange for Ellen when Linda put her arm around her shoulder and said with tears in her eyes, "Oh, Ellen, my husband left me and built a house with this woman he had been seeing. And he ruined my life and our kids' lives."

Surprised, Ellen replied, "Oh, dear, Linda. When did this happen?"

"Ten years ago," Linda answered.

Ellen was shocked that Linda was still so devastated and was living in that painful moment. As her Genius technician called her name, Linda said, "I don't know what your story is, but I hope this doesn't ruin your life and your kids' lives."

Ellen had wanted to tell Linda that her own situation wasn't going to ruin her life or the lives of her kids. She confided to me that when driving home from the Apple Store, she wanted to believe that no person or circumstance had the power to ruin her life or her kids' lives or even her ex-husband's, for that matter.

Ellen mentioned that she felt sorry for Linda—not necessarily for what happened with her ex-husband but because she seemed to be stuck in despair and remained fixated on it. She wondered later if, in a spirit of friendship, she should have pointed out that Linda might be caught up in her own *Groundhog Day*, reliving the hurt over and over each day as if it just happened.

Jane Austen tells us that it doesn't have to be this way. There is another approach. Ellen and Linda represented two opposing Austen archetypes, who offered us different ways to respond to life upheaval. We could wade in the deluge of our suffering, or we could start to swim. This was the difference between pragmatic Elinor Dashwood and her anguished sister, Marianne.

Marianne Dashwood, like her mother, cannot accept the death of her father and the way her stepbrother John, persuaded by his greedy wife, refused to honor his promise to his dying father to financially care for his stepmother and stepsisters, who have been left comparatively penniless and homeless. In describing Marianne and Mrs. Dashwood's "excess of . . . sensibility,"[9] grief, anguish, despair, Jane Austen writes,

> They encouraged each other now in the violence of their affliction. The agony of grief which overpowered them at first, was voluntarily renewed, was sought for, was created again and again. They gave themselves up wholly to their sorrow, seeking increase of wretchedness in every reflection that could afford it, and resolved against ever admitting consolation in future.[10]

Patricia Meyer Spacks and David Shapard have noted that Marianne and Mrs. Dashwood resemble one another in their anguish and grief[11] and in their "conscious indulgence in misery."[12] Given all the hardship and trauma they have endured, it might seem harsh to talk about a conscious indulgence in misery, but according to Stuart Tave, Jane Austen suggests that Marianne and Mrs. Dashwood's fixation with their despair is "a deliberate moral choice, and a choice of weakness. . . . [T]heir sensibility . . . overpowers them and is voluntarily renewed, sought for, and created again and again."[13]

If Elizabeth Bennet is the exemplar of accepting *who* we are, then Elinor Dashwood epitomizes the importance of accepting *where* we are, no matter how traumatic or difficult. As Shapard has said, unlike her sister and mother, "even in this, the greatest emotional trial she has faced, Elinor still rationally accepts the facts."[14] Elinor is resilience personified. Resilience is just as essential in work as it is in the personal sphere. Former *Harvard Business Review* senior editor Diana Coutu describes the characteristics of resilient leaders, which are summarized as follows:

> Resilient people possess three defining characteristics: They coolly accept the harsh realities facing them. They find meaning in terrible times. And they have an uncanny ability to improvise, making do with whatever's at hand.[15]

Aside from the fact that she's an uneducated nineteen-year-old fictional character, that description remarkably echoes how Austen first presents Elinor to us in *Sense and Sensibility*:

> Elinor, this eldest daughter whose advice was so effectual, possessed a strength of understanding, and coolness of judgment, which qualified her, though only nineteen, to be the counsellor of her mother, and enabled her frequently to counteract, to the advantage of them all, that eagerness of mind in Mrs. Dashwood which must generally have led to imprudence.[16]

Prudential leadership in life and in business is integral to success. Effective leaders do not "slip into denial" to cope with hardship. Rather they take "very sober and down-to-earth views" of the reality of the situation.[17] Elinor was so good at doing this.

Elinor, too, was deeply afflicted; but still she could struggle, she could exert herself. She could consult with her brother, could receive her sister-in-law on her arrival, and treat her with proper attention; and could strive to rouse her mother to similar exertion, and encourage her to similar forbearance.[18]

Elinor's resilience and acceptance of their plight does not mean she does not feel the grief, anguish, and fear that her mother and sister do.

She had an excellent heart;—her disposition was affectionate, and her feelings were strong; but she knew how to govern them: it was a knowledge which her mother had yet to learn; and which one of her sisters had resolved never to be taught.[19]

Elinor utilizes several strategies to manage her grief, but the first one is a kind of radical acceptance of where they are. As David Shapard has said, "even in ... the greatest emotional trial she has faced, Elinor still rationally accepts the facts."[20] What distinguishes Elinor and an internally referenced leader is that they accept where they are in the present moment instead of being preoccupied with the awful thing that happened in the past or the terrible thing that might happen in the future. Ellen Langer, professor of psychology at Harvard University and founder of the Langer Mindfulness Institute, explains that "mindfulness is the process of actively noticing new things [and] when you do that, it puts you in the present." She urges leaders to stay present in the current moment in order to avoid the "stressful ... mindless negative evaluations we make and the worry that we'll find problems and not be able to solve them."[21] For Langer and internally referenced leaders, staying grounded and present are key attributes of effective leadership.

Elinor is fully present in the moment. In contrast, both Marianne and her mother are fixated on the past as well as the future.

This applies even to events that may bode well for them, such as Marianne meeting the handsome Willoughby. When Willoughby rescues Marianne, swooping her up on his white horse after her fall in the rain, Jane Austen tells us that "her imagination was busy, her reflections were pleasant, and the pain of a sprained ancle [sic] was disregarded."[22] Almost from that very first encounter with Willoughby, Marianne and her mother were living in an idealized future.

> Her mother too, in whose mind not one speculative thought of their marriage had been raised, by his prospect of riches, was led before the end of a week to hope and expect it; and secretly to congratulate herself on having gained two such sons-in-law as Edward and Willoughby.[23]

Whether it's an agonizing past or an idealized future, Marianne and Mrs. Dashwood are overcome by the pendulum swing of overwhelming emotions; they hardly accept, let alone live, in the present moment. Ironically, they are perpetually stuck in whatever strong emotions they are experiencing about the past or future and can, thus, never move beyond any crisis or elation.

Elinor, on the other hand, was able to acknowledge where they were as a family, without bitterness about what happened to them and without anxiety about what was to come. Only with present radical acceptance—reconciling herself to a difficult situation without resistance—was Elinor able to move past their situation. That is the crucial first step in cultivating an internally referenced leader's path toward resilience. The internally referenced leader is able to soberly accept where she is in the present moment without judgment or blame. She holds her strong emotions at bay so that she can dispassionately accept where she is now.

In the seminal leadership book *The 7 Habits of Highly Effective People*, author Stephen Covey talks about how critical it is to "accept those things that at present we can't control, while we focus our efforts on the things that we can."[24] Covey emphasizes the importance of learning from the past but not living in the past. For him, it is about learning from a difficult situation and accepting it so that one can move beyond it. To illustrate this process of letting go of past difficulties and being able to reset, Covey describes how when one of his sons was a college quarterback, he "learned to snap his wristband between plays as a kind of mental checkoff whenever he or anyone made a *setting back* mistake, so the last mistake wouldn't affect the resolve and execution of the next play."[25] For Covey and for Austen in her depiction of Elinor Dashwood, it is a constant choice and a disciplined practice to accept the present moment and move forward.

Detached "Coolness of Judgment"

Possessing "a strength of understanding and coolness of judgment" empowers leaders to deal with any situation no matter how difficult. As an internally referenced leader, detachment is an absolutely necessary technology in times of crisis.

Heidi, a grief coach affiliated with the Memory Circle and ALTAR, works with people in crisis. She utilizes her professional and personal experience with trauma to help individuals process and overcome devastating losses. Before guiding her clients to constructively process the intensity of their strong emotions, she sometimes urges them to detach first. Heidi says that "detachment is misunderstood and gets a bad rap these days." She explains that "some people think of detaching from strong feelings as not having feelings, hiding feelings, or pushing feelings down. Some people think of it as disengaging with the world, tuning the world out, and shutting it off." For Heidi, however, being able to detach from strong feelings in the moment is crucial for some of her clients so that they can "create the time and space they need that may be more conducive for processing those overwhelming feelings, especially while having to attend to the demands and needs of daily life."[26]

Leadership experts also talk about the importance of being able to detach from strong feelings during times of disruptive change. Ronald Heifetz, codirector of the Center for Public Leadership at Harvard University's Kennedy School of Government, and his colleague Marty Linsky of Cambridge Leadership Associates describe the need for leaders to "operate in and above the fray"[27] during times of intense change. The metaphor they employ to describe being able to separate oneself from the turmoil is "getting off the dance floor and going to the balcony," where a leader can more objectively observe from a distance.[28] They say that being able to observe as well as participate and move back and forth between those states of detachment and engagement empower a leader with a calm ability to be able to maintain perspective and the capacity to reflect.[29] Heifetz and Linsky acknowledge that removing oneself from the fray is "extremely tough to do when . . . fiercely engaged down below, being pushed and pulled by . . . events and people," which is why it is an important leadership skill to develop.[30]

Elinor Dashwood may be a fictional character, but Austen portrays her as someone who has mastered operating above the fray. Elinor's healthy detachment enables her to create space for a thorough understanding of the situation. From that space and understanding, she can make rational decisions—not just for herself but also for her family and her community—about how best to move forward and how to effectively engage in the world. Detachment is one of Elinor Dashwood's great strengths and a skill that an internally referenced leader needs in order to move forward with resilience.

Unlike Marianne, Elinor does not react to new situations with immediate intense emotionality and reactive judgment. As Shapard notes, Elinor "is consistently shown taking time and care in her evaluations of others, and her judgments usually prove to be more accurate."[31] Moreover, "Elinor is not simply relying on her own feelings, but supplementing them with other people's perceptions and opinions."[32] Shapard has described this as "intellectual caution."[33] In other words, she is "influenced by her heart" but "does not judge solely by it."[34] Similarly, Spacks notes,

> Elinor often speaks . . . , even in intimate conversation, in rather formal fashion, making a case for her view of the world and the people in it. Moreland Perkins declares her "an intellectual" because of her "unrelenting, dispassionate, analytical inquiry into the causes, contents, contexts, and outcomes of individual persons' conduct and experience."[35]

It is not that the internally referenced leader like Elinor does not have intense feelings, a strong gut instinct, or a distinct point of view. Rather, she forces herself to detach and view the situation from a more objective witness space so that she can calmly and coolly assess the situation and make the best unbiased decisions for herself, her family, and her community.

Renee, a police officer also earning a doctoral degree in our educational leadership program at DePaul, exemplifies the detached controlled composure of Elinor Dashwood. In describing her promotion denial, which she thought might have been based on race and gender, she was calm, cerebral, and rational. In response to my stupefied reaction, she explained,

> It's always necessary to pause and calm down, whether dealing with potential crime on the streets or the nonsense of the old boys network at the force who are threatened by an African

American woman who wants to change some paradigms. This doesn't mean I'm not angry, frustrated, or sometimes even hopeless. But I have to keep myself together. It is the only way to make real progress.[36]

A detached internally referenced leader may give the impression that she is made of stone, but her composed demeanor is only a strategy for moving forward in the most calm and intentional way possible. For the internally referenced leader, acceptance, detachment, and letting go are the necessary components of the resilience she needs to not only survive trauma but ultimately transcend it.

When I describe Elinor's detachment as a necessary part of internally referenced leadership, many students and clients say that one is either cool under pressure or not. A woman who stepped down from an assistant principalship because of the stress of the job protested that being calm "is an attribute over which we have little control."[37] Jane Austen, however, would disagree. Through her daily practice of exertion, Elinor Dashwood forces herself to practice detachment in most situations.

She Knew How to Govern Them

"Her feelings were strong; but she knew how to govern them," which enabled her to act with a "cool" head. As an internally referenced leader, you regularly utilize exertion to keep strong feelings at bay in order to be as effective as possible.

Though Marianne calls her sister Elinor "cold-hearted,"[38] she was anything but. In fact, Austen tells us that Elinor "had an excellent heart."[39] This process of being calm in spite of strong feelings and in spite of adverse conditions is how Elinor can inform the internally referenced leader every day. Austen describes

Elinor's struggle to keep her strong feeling at bay most acutely when she learns about how the man she loves, Edward Ferrars, has been secretly engaged to the manipulative Lucy Steele.

> Elinor saw that it *was* his hand, and she could doubt no longer.
> . . . [F]or a few moments, she was almost overcome—her heart sunk [*sic*] within her, and she could hardly stand; but exertion was indispensably necessary, and she struggled so resolutely against the oppression of her feelings, that her success was speedy, and for the time complete.[40]

Writing about this passage and Elinor's struggle, Patricia Meyer Spacks observes, "This scene offers abundant evidence of Elinor's sensibility, her capacity for strong feeling. She endures great, and increasing, emotion, although her ethos and habit of self-discipline prevent her from openly revealing it."[41] The self-discipline she uses to stay calm in spite of strong feelings and great challenges is labeled by Austen as *exertion*.

Many scholars have concluded that Elinor is admirable because, despite the intensity of her emotions, she is able to exert herself over those strong feelings and keep them in check so they do not overtake her and interfere with her ability to function and keep her family moving forward. Spacks elucidates Austen's use of *exertion* in distinguishing Elinor's extraordinary mental effort and its significance in the novel:

> "Exertion" is frequently associated with Elinor in the course of the novel; it may be yet more important than *sense* as a key to her character. Sense, to be sure, often provides the cause of her exertion, but she exerts herself ceaselessly—not only to conceal her feelings, from Lucy and her family, but also to keep social machinery running smoothly and to protect herself from various forms of intrusion. Her capacity for exertion and her

will to exert herself differentiate her from all the novel's other characters.[42]

Thus, for Elinor and the internally referenced leader, exertion over strong emotion is not a skill that necessarily comes easily; nor is it a onetime occurrence. Rather, it comes from steadfast self-discipline and requires practice on a daily basis. No matter how passionate Elinor feels, she does not allow the intensity of those feelings to dictate her actions.

Jennifer is one of the most Elinor-Dashwoodesque and effective school administrators who ever attended DePaul's graduate program in educational leadership. She attended our master's program to become a principal and then our doctoral program to become a superintendent. When I first met her years ago, she was the assistant principal of Roosevelt High School in Chicago. The phrase "multitask on steroids" does not begin to describe what she was like when we met to collaborate on a variety of programs. Many of our meetings were at the school where she was working. She would talk to me about scheduling and the curriculum of our onsite cohort and at the same time, through an earpiece, listen to the school social worker inform her about the whereabouts of a distraught sophomore. And then, without missing a beat, she would pick up the conversation exactly where we left off.

I have always been impressed with Jenn's calm, detached demeanor, no matter how fraught the situation. It was not surprising that several years later she was promoted to principal of an elementary school in one of the most impoverished areas of Chicago. Again, she had to deal with many angry, frustrated stakeholders. She was an excellent principal and turned that school around academically in a remarkably short time. Her fame around the district, however, was fully cemented when she stood her ground and kept calm dealing with the problem of gun violence that was circling her school. Since Jenn had started her education career as a school social worker, it was through this prism that she advocated bringing mental health support and safety training to the community, instead of calling in the police. Someone remarked that Jenn was made of steel. When I disagreed, my colleague clarified: "I meant it as a compliment, Andrea. She can handle anything. That is what the best leaders we know are made of."[43]

People who have the uncanny ability to be calm and to solve problems with emotional detachment are not necessarily made of steel. They are not robots. Often the opposite is true. Because Jennifer cares so much about her students and their families and the social injustices they face, it requires a lot of discipline to keep her fear, sadness, anger, and worry at bay so that she can calmly and coolly problem-solve with them to create a better school and a better community.

She has since been promoted to superintendent. We met recently to discuss her dissertation, and I could tell something was wrong. She couldn't focus on her research; and for once, she couldn't multitask. Holding back tears, she told me,

> I ran into one of my former students from my principal days. He asked if I was in charge. When I nodded, he told me that he didn't feel safe at school. He also told me that his older sibling had been shot and the teacher didn't seem to care.[44]

Jennifer cared. In fact, the traumatic impact of adverse childhood experiences was her dissertation study. Tears welled up as she told me that her former student's story "had hit home." She was not made of steel after all.

So how do internally referenced leaders like Jennifer exert themselves on a daily basis over strong feelings and difficult circumstances without becoming paralyzed, disillusioned, or utterly depleted? Jennifer says that when things get very tense, she has this ability to "hit pause like on a DVR and be calm, quiet, and still until the right action appears" and then she "presses play" and resumes. Similar to Elinor, she exerts by being *in* the situation but not *of* the situation. Watching the drama from a dispassionate vantage point, she can calm down, clearly understand what's going on, and rationally generate solutions for all interested stakeholders.

This ability to witness from a place of objectivity, beyond emotion, is a practice that leadership experts describe. They use some interesting metaphors to illustrate the ability to remove to a place of objective detachment, where the internally referenced leader can zoom out to view their circumstances and emotions from a safe distance rather than overly identify and risk being consumed. The first image is recommended by conflict resolution guru William Ury. He writes about how—just like Austen shows with Elinor—even in the midst of the greatest conflict and strife, we can always choose to be calm, to be detached, to not be overcome by strong feelings and difficult situations. He also describes this in a powerful metaphor about a dispassionate place of witness called Going to the Balcony:

> We have a choice. We don't need to react. We can learn to observe ourselves instead. In my teaching and writing, I emphasize the concept of *going to the balcony*. The balcony is a metaphor for a mental and emotional place of perspective, calm, and self-control. If life is a stage and we are all actors on that stage, then the balcony is a place from which we can see the entire play unfolding with greater clarity. To observe our selves, it is valuable to go the balcony at all times, and especially before, during, and after any problematic conversation or negotiation.[45]

He talks about how learning to observe ourselves is "simple, but not easy" and "with practice, [we] get better and better. Ideally, the balcony is not just a place to visit from time to time, but rather a home base."[46] As an internally referenced leader, Jennifer has practiced and cultivated using this balcony space as her home base, which has enabled her to exert herself over strong feelings and difficult circumstances day in and day out.

From the balcony, the internally referenced leader can perceive the whole of the situation with a calm resilience and disciplined exertion; she is then able to not just survive but thrive as she makes rational decisions for herself and her organization. Jennifer said that her ability to distance herself and stay calm and reflective during crises has also influenced how she works with and trains her faculty and staff. Committed to the belief that the only way "to make any effective decision is from a safe emotional distance," she engages in professional development with her team so that the organizations she leads have cultures that are "responsive and not reactive."[47]

This higher-level view is what Jennifer endeavors to instill in her leadership team so that they can view themselves as detached but empowered managers rather than as embroiled, passive workers. Because of her background working on mental health issues, she seeks to provide multifaceted support to ensure that high emotions do not get in the way of clear decision making. This support includes employing a helpful response team, whose members inherently have a more detached perspective because they do not work in the school building where the crisis occurred. Jennifer also provides emotional support for any principal who needs help processing intense emotions. To ensure that no high-stakes decisions are made in a heightened emotional state, everyone is encouraged to wait twenty-four hours before acting, whenever possible, in order to minimize reactivity.

Still, she admits that there are times when it is very difficult to detach. She mentions the time a young boy came to her office saying that "there was a weapon in the house." Gun violence permeates the boy's neighborhood and even home. "There was no space where he felt safe—even in school, and that is unacceptable," she said. This incident and all the gun violence in the area where her schools are located, along with the trauma it inflicts, make her feel "angry and powerless." Jennifer says that at these times, she needs to "find her Zen."

When going to the balcony doesn't work, try coming at it this way: Buddhist philosopher Thich Nhat Hanh's tree in a storm metaphor. He writes,

> When we're overcome by strong emotions[,] we're like a tree in a storm, with its top branches and leaves swaying in the wind. But the trunk of the tree is solid, stable, and deeply rooted in the earth. When we're caught in a storm of emotions, we can practice to be like the trunk of the tree. We don't stay up in the high branches. We go down to the trunk and become still, not carried away by our thinking and emotions. . . . [W]e just focus all our attention on the rise and fall of our abdomen, our trunk.[48]

Obviously, Elinor Dashwood didn't do breathwork at a Buddhist retreat, but she does seem to embody that breath, that pause, that trunk that so many of us try to practice now. Staying grounded and calm in the trunk is what enables internally referenced leaders to hunker down and weather even the most violent storm with grace and equanimity. While the internally referenced leader cannot shape the existence, the duration, or the impact of the storm, by staying in her trunk, she can manage her response to it. This gives her a kind of control over the seemingly uncontrollable. Spacks makes the point that Elinor's self-control is the only influence she has in a chaotic world; therefore her ability to remove herself emotionally is a source of power.[49]

In Jennifer's case, she was able to ultimately gain a sense of control by researching the topic of childhood trauma in schools for her dissertation and exploring how leaders can proactively and intentionally design strategic systems to support all stakeholders impacted by trauma. Jennifer has been using her research in groundbreaking ways to inform the administrators and teachers she supervises about best practices for working with students who have been impacted by early trauma. It's a topic she has spoken about at several education conferences.

At times, however, the internally referenced leader does get swept up in the emotion, which can be beautiful as long as it is done in a way that does not undermine the leader, her family, or her organization. In a poignant scene at the end of *Sense and Sensibility*, Elinor, after many trials, unexpectedly and miraculously discovers that Edward is now free to follow his heart. Edward is available and in love with Elinor (he has been all this time), and she is in love with him. He is about to propose, and Elinor is overwrought with emotion. As he comes up the stairs to their cottage, she says to herself, "I *will* be calm! I *will* be mistress of myself!"[50]

I *will* be calm. I *will* be in my trunk. I *will* go to the balcony. I *will* get through this. I *will* breathe and detach and watch and wait and calmly step forward. We've been on an emotional journey with Elinor: in order to be resilient for her family's survival, she has had to hold her feelings in. Then when she finally gets to a safe place where she can fully express them, we are deeply moved as she bursts into "tears of joy which . . . she thought would never cease."[51] As Tave explains this scene,

> Elinor's emotions are not less than Marianne's; that they do not come as easily and violently as Marianne's. . . . [T]he attempt to control and conceal, rather than encourage and display them,

gives them a greater integrity and force, more feeling sensibility. Her emotions are greater than Marianne's and her exertions are greater.

She is now obliged to "unceasing exertion" by the necessity of concealing what she has been told.[52]

An uncharacteristically giddy and joyful Jennifer recently mentioned that she was working on a grant to partner with an organization called Mindful Practices to provide mindfulness and trauma-informed training for stakeholders in her schools and even to the surrounding community. Like Jennifer and Elinor, the internally referenced leader has strong emotions but knows how to exert so that she can go from scared to objective and then, when conditions have stabilized, express those well-earned tears.

So Calm So Cheerful

For an internally referenced leader, reframing problems as opportunities enables the focusing on solutions.

Elinor accepts, detaches, and exerts with a remarkably good attitude given the difficult circumstances she faces. Emily Auerbach explains that if "Marianne illustrates the unbridled zeal of French revolutionaries, perhaps Elinor embodies the enduring British tradition of remaining composed under pressure, of keeping a stiff upper lip. Passages describing Elinor are dotted with words like *judgment, reason, duty, principle, observation, thought, restraint, command, civility, decorum,* and *knowledge.*"[53]

Auerbach writes about how Elinor's "calm, steady, reasoned judgment" keeps "her family functional throughout the novel."[54] One of the most moving dialogues between Marianne and Elinor comes when Marianne discovers how Elinor has been holding onto her terrible, painful secret and all the while taking care of her sisters and mother.

"Four months!"—cried Marianne again.—"So calm!—so cheerful!—how have you been supported?"—

   "By feeling that I was doing my duty....

   ... I would not have you suffer on my account; for I assure you I no longer suffer materially myself. I have many things to support me."[55]

Like Elinor, the internally referenced leader aims to be calm and cool but also cheerful or at least focuses on positive aspects, even when times are difficult or even when there might be contradictory feelings inside. At the very least, a positive pragmatic lens might enable her to reframe her story and focus on solutions rather than problems.

Leadership experts confirm that this positive reframing is not necessarily easy or natural. In fact, according to Harvard Business School experts Joshua Margolis and Paul Stoltz, it is a discipline that requires daily practice and what they call a "resilience regimen" in order "to help managers replace negative responses with creative, resourceful ones and to move forward despite real or perceived obstacles."[56] They talk about the importance of changing from passive "Cause-Oriented Thinking" (victim thinking) to "active ... Response-Oriented Thinking" so that instead of asking why an adverse event happened, we ask how the situation can improve and how we can "contain the negatives ... and generate currently unseen positives?"[57]

It takes discipline to reframe difficult circumstances into opportunities, whether those events are professional or personal and no matter how challenging or devastating those events might be. Viktor Frankl, Holocaust survivor, psychiatrist, and founder of Logotherapy, famously describes this ability in his groundbreaking book *Man's Search for Meaning*. In German, his book is entitled *Trotzdem Ja zum Leben sagen: Ein Psychologe erlebt das Konzentrationslager*, which translates to "Saying Yes to Life in

Spite of Everything: A Psychologist Experiences the Concentration Camp."[58]

Frankl observed that some of his fellow prisoners were able to find meaning and purpose even in the midst of the most extreme brutality, devastation, and despair. He explains that "the way they bore their suffering was a genuine inner achievement. It is this spiritual freedom—which cannot be taken away—that makes life meaningful and purposeful."[59] Frankl witnessed how forces beyond our control can take everything away except for our ability to perceive our own situation. For him, there is real agency, power, and freedom in this. As he writes, "it is not freedom from conditions, but it *is* freedom to take a stand toward the conditions."[60]

Like Elinor Dashwood, the internally referenced leader knows she cannot necessarily control conditions, but she can always control her response to them. She has faith that even if currently she doesn't understand the purpose, meaning, and positive aspects of a challenging situation, she *will* be able to understand eventually.

Breast cancer survivor and internally referenced leader Kathy Bresler says, "My diagnosis completely upended my life and was the best thing that ever happened to me." Indeed, Kathy's life changed dramatically when she found out she was sick. She viewed this as an opportunity to reconsider how she spent her time and what she wanted to do. She had been an effective business leader as a strategy consultant at Bain Consulting and had an MBA from Northwestern's Kellogg School of Management. While she always enjoyed her career in business, she says that she felt as though her "work self and real self were two different people." For years, she had been secretly studying her passion, which involved empowering women, but she had been hesitant about actually pursuing it. The moment after she received her cancer diagnosis, however, everything seemed possible. She held this ostensibly difficult news as an incredible life opening. She describes her feelings this way:

> On Friday afternoon I got a call and they said you have invasive ductal carcinoma. I went down to my office. I noticed my first feeling was relief. It was really odd but I could feel it was relief. It was permission to drop the outside expectations, the perfectionism, the idea of success that increasingly did not feel like me. There was a relief in that. It became incredibly joyful in a weird way. I found my voice and heart. It sucks to go through chemo and lose my hair. But at the same time, it was expansiveness and freedom and heartful connectivity as long as I saw this as being for me.[61]

So many people, understandably, would be angry, afraid, confused, and unsure about a cancer diagnosis. Kathy, however, viewed it as an opportunity to follow her heart and find out what really mattered to her. By holding her diagnosis as something that was happening *for* her instead of *to* her, it became a tremendous catalyst for personal growth and a personal renaissance. With her brave and positive "how is this for me" perspective, Kathy did not just make the best of having cancer, but she utilized her cancer to create the best outcomes for herself and those around her.

As Kathy was realizing that she did not want to return to the business world, she learned that Northwestern University Hospital had received a grant and was looking for a part-time marketing person. As it turned out, she was the ideal candidate: the position required a breast cancer survivor who could conduct one-on-one interviews and focus groups with cancer survivors and their families to describe their experiences going through treatment and its aftermath. Kathy says that she "came alive" working with these women and learning about what they needed in order to

feel whole and transcendent. Most importantly, she also realized that she "was much more interested in the empowerment
and positive side of things and not so much pathology." She became determined to help larger groups of women "live fully and
authentically."[62]

Kathy worked with Seena Frost to become a certified Soul
Collage facilitator. Seena, a Jungian psychotherapist who had
studied theology at Yale Divinity School, developed a personal
empowerment tool using archetypes and self-inquiry to heighten
one's intuitive knowledge and sense of personal agency. As her
Soul Collage clientele expanded, Kathy founded Tend Your Soul,
which offers group and individual empowerment programs. She
also collaborated with intuitive leadership coach Susan Hyman
to create women's empowerment circles called LIFT, which
stands for "Living in Flow Together." Kathy and Susan say that
the mission statement of LIFT is to establish "an emerging cocre-
ative community of women coming together for the *soul* purpose
of creating more possibility in their lives, their work, and their
world."[63]

LIFT has been so effective that Kathy moved it from her living
room to a large space in Chicago called ALTAR. She finds it ex-
traordinarily gratifying to help participants reframe challenging
situations into experiences of growth and transcendence. At the
end of LIFT sessions, women stand in a circle and hold hands.
And one woman to the next, we say, *that which is right is unfolding*. Like Kathy, many women in the circle are dealing with cancer, abuse, sick children, bankruptcy, divorce, sexual harassment,
and other difficult life challenges. And yet, she says to these same
people, *that which is right is unfolding*; and we say it to ourselves
no matter what state we are in. It is LIFT's spiritual practice and
discipline. She says, "Even if they don't understand why they are
going through something, the positive reframe is that it will make

sense at some point in the future and they will learn and grow and get to a better place." Kathy has recently been ordained as an interfaith minister from One Spirit Seminary in New York because of this unrelenting faith.

One of Kathy's mentors, Kathleen Medina, talks about swimming unfettered with the current of life. She says, "If we try to keep holding on, our fingers will eventually be pried. But if we can move with the current and trust it is taking us to some place better, we will experience transcendence at some point. And even the act of surrendering to the journey is in itself transcendence."[64]

Like Elinor Dashwood, Kathy, with unwavering discipline, cheerfully goes with life and trusts that it is ultimately happening for her, no matter how challenging. This is her spiritual practice.

How to Put More Elinor in Your Life

We can put more Elinor in our lives by accepting difficult realities instead of avoiding them, denying them, and pushing them away. The only way to move past something is to acknowledge that it exists. The ability to detach from strong emotions and use exertion to keep them at bay enables us to function in the midst of crisis. It is important, however, that we express and process our impassioned reactions when we again find ourselves on solid ground. Finally, we reframe challenges as opportunities, enabling us to focus on solutions rather than problems and to find meaning on our long (sometimes hard) journey to growth.

Exercises for Operationalizing Principle 2

1. X Marks the Spot: Map Your Location for Radical Acceptance.

Use paper to write or draw a difficult place you might be in. (Unemployed, Divorced, Health Issues, etc.) Write or draw where you are in terms of facts rather than opinions. For example, instead of saying, *My greedy boss screwed me over and let me go*, say *On March 1, I received notice that my position was being eliminated as of April 1.* Knowing where you are on the map, as objectively as possible, enables you to focus on setting your course for someplace else: a better place.

2. Create a Calming Mantra.

In order to stay calm amidst the most agonizing crisis, Elinor used the mantra, "I *will* be calm! I *will* be mistress of myself!" Create a mantra for yourself—not to deny your feelings but to calm yourself so they don't overtake you. Perhaps it is what you would say to soothe that fearful overwrought inner child who is having a tantrum or panic attack. What can you say to calm her down?

3. Go to the Balcony to See Possibilities.

What is your biggest worry at the moment? Write one page about it. Take out a red pen and cross out all words that are evaluations and judgments, such as, bad, good, hopeless, or terrible. Now cross out all words that are opinions rather than facts. For example, *my irresponsible husband, Dan, wasted fifty thousand dollars on that risky investment* would become *Dan invested fifty thousand dollars, which is now worth fifty dollars*. From the balcony, how can you reframe to focus on possible solutions?

4. Worst Day or Best Day? You Choose.

Close your eyes and recall one of the most challenging times of your life. It's okay if it brings up pain and sorrow and anger and devastation. Feel it all. But as you look at it from where you are now, can you find some good in it? How was it *for* you? How did it help you grow? How did it lead to something better? How did it help you create appreciation for what you still have or what you got in response to it? What were the moments of kindness and love that seemed so poignant in the midst of your crisis? How has it helped you become the person you are now?

3

In Defense of Sea-Faring Folks with Weathered Skin

Like Anne Elliot from *Persuasion*, choose, create, and claim paradigms based on internal worthiness, hard work, and merit over external constructs that bestow the shortcuts of privilege, entitlement, and membership in the "right" club.

Meet Anne Elliot

In *Persuasion*, Anne Elliot's family is forced to leave their home because of the reckless spending of her father, Sir Walter Elliot, whose "vanity was the beginning and the end"[1] of his character. He resents the fact that he is forced to rent his family's aristocratic estate to self-made Admiral Croft, whose profession Sir Walter disdains, in part because of "what a sea-faring life can do" to a man's appearance: "I know it is the same with them all: they are all knocked about, and exposed to every climate, and every weather, till they are not fit to be seen."[2] Like their father, Sir Walter's oldest and youngest daughters are vain, shallow, and entitled. His middle daughter, Anne, however, is quite different: "no one [was] so proper, so capable as Anne"[3] with her "gentleness, modesty, taste, and feeling."[4] Anne resembled their worthy and hardworking late mother, who had run their household with "method, moderation, and economy."[5]

In addition to losing her mother, Anne experiences several other significant losses throughout the course of the novel. Her selfish father requires her, rather than her sisters, to maintain and ultimately transition their household, but he never has a kind word to say to her or about her, explicitly shunning her and favoring her self-absorbed older sister. More poignantly, Anne loses an early romantic relationship with Frederick Wentworth, whose sister is married to Admiral Croft. Anne and Frederick had been engaged eight years earlier, but Sir Walter and her godmother, Lady Russell, persuaded her to break it off because they deemed it "a very degrading alliance,"[6] given her aristocratic family and his lack of connections.

After his "honourable toils" in the war, Frederick Wentworth comes back into Anne's life as a wealthy and heroic captain in the navy. *Persuasion* explores this rare and precious second chance for Anne and Frederick and the possibility of "just rewards" for two hardworking, worthy souls.[7]

Vanity Was the Beginning and the End

The most effective leaders are "sea-faring folks with weathered skin," who work hard for their success rather than having it handed to them at birth. As an internally referenced leader, you prefer hard work and merit over privilege and entitlement.

Greta Thunberg may be just five feet tall, but she is a tour de force, who at seventeen has been a climate activist since she was a little girl. What began as skipping school on Fridays to protest outside the Swedish parliament has transformed into a global movement. Thunberg has traveled throughout the world to meet with global leaders and address preeminent conferences and assemblies about the climate crisis. She does not consider her Asperger's diagnosis a liability—in fact, she calls it her "superpower." She is unafraid to proclaim her clarion call with unequivocal directness, clarity, and understandable derision.

Greta does not mince words. In a speech to the European Economic and Social Committee on February 21, 2019, entitled "You're Acting Like Spoiled, Irresponsible Children," Greta admonishes the politicians and privileged who have caused, contributed to, and ignored the climate crisis:

> You can't just sit around waiting for hope to come; you're acting like spoiled, irresponsible children. You don't seem to understand that hope is something you have to earn. And if you still say that we are wasting valuable lesson time, then let me remind you that our political leaders have wasted decades through denial and inaction. And since our time is running out, we have decided to take action. We have started to clean up your mess and we will not stop until we are done.[8]

She suggests that when it comes to climate change, unexpectedly, it is her generation that prefers hard work, merit, and accountability while an older generation of adult politicians displays entitlement, privilege, and flagrant irresponsibility.

Anne Elliot's voice is not as strong as Greta Thunberg's, but her work ethic is. She too prefers a paradigm based on hard work and accountability. In *Persuasion* the two contrasting paradigms of leadership, privilege and entitlement versus hard work and merit, are also found in the corporate world, in the political world, and in almost every other realm. The question to ask, in all these environments, is whether we want to work for and with people like the industrious, intelligent Admiral and Mrs. Croft or people like the shallow and entitled Sir Walter Elliot and his equally vacuous older daughter. I choose the Crofts every time. I choose the internally referenced leader every time.

Jane Austen opens *Persuasion* by introducing us to Sir Walter Elliot. He's reading his favorite book, the aristocratic *Baronetage*, of course, preoccupied with the entry about him and his aristocratic heritage. Austen's description of him recalls a modern leadership paradigm we are all too familiar with when she writes,

> Vanity was the beginning and the end of Sir Walter Elliot's character; vanity of person and of situation. He had been remarkably handsome in his youth; and, at fifty-four, was still a very fine man. Few women could think more of their personal appearance than he did; nor could the valet of any new made lord be more delighted with the place he held in society. He considered the blessing of beauty as inferior only to the blessing of a baronetcy; and the Sir Walter Elliot, who united these gifts, was the constant object of his warmest respect and devotion.[9]

With such a vain personality, it was mortifying to him that he had to rent his estate to the newly wealthy, decorated, and weathered Admiral Croft. This was entirely Elliot's own doing, based on his poor management of his estate and his profligate spending and completely selfish, thoughtless ways. He would never admit his mistakes, but he fiercely objected to the arrangement with Admiral Croft:

> I have two strong grounds of objection to it. First, as being the means of bringing persons of obscure birth into undue distinction, and raising men to honours which their fathers and grandfathers never dreamt of; and secondly, as it cuts up a man's youth . . . a sailor grows old sooner than any other man. I have observed it all my life. A man is in greater danger in the navy of being insulted by the rise of one whose father, his father might

have disdained to speak to, and of becoming prematurely an object of disgust himself, than in any other line . . . the most deplorable-looking personage you can imagine, his face the colour of mahogany, rough and rugged to the last degree, all lines and wrinkles.[10]

Sir Walter resented these naval officers who made fortunes based on their service, many of whom not only were decorated but were also given noble titles. Robert Morrison explains that many admirals "came from the lower ranks of society, and their ascension to the peerage was a source of considerable irritation to conservatives such as Sir Walter Elliot."[11] Sir Walter reviled these worthy men who rose through the ranks through their own merit and achievement, weathering many storms at sea on behalf of country. He showed "contempt for their relative newness"[12] as well as for their lack of aristocratic heritage and good skin.

Persuasion is a novel that is largely shaped by war and those who fought hard, sacrificed, and were victorious for the whole country. In fact, Austen began writing *Persuasion* on the day that Napoleon was sent into exile, August 8, 1815. Because Britain relied heavily on its navy for protection, there was "an unwillingness to promote less qualified people just because of their social background."[13] This upended the social order and put more value on merit and hard work than on entitlement and privilege. The defeat of Napoleon and the threat of future conflict loom large in *Persuasion* and suggest the need for talented, brave, hardworking navy men and the advent of a more progressive social hierarchy based on industry, talent, contribution, and individual worthiness.

According to Morrison's annotations,

Further difficulties arise for Sir Walter when . . . he cannot keep himself out of serious debt, and . . . is forced to move to

Bath after renting Kellynch to Admiral Croft, a highly successful naval officer who has amassed a considerable sum in prize
money, and who fought alongside Lord Nelson at the Battle of
Trafalgar. Although he does not fully comprehend it, Sir Walter's life changed dramatically in the year of the French Revolu-
tion, while that same event gave men such as Admiral Croft the
opportunity to make their fortune and to advance far up the
social scale through merit and courage.[14]

The first words of Anne Elliot in *Persuasion* reveal that she
admires the hard work and talent of those in service. She says,
"The Navy, I think, who have done so much for us, have at least an
equal claim with any other set of men, for all the comforts and all
the privileges which any home can give. Sailors work hard enough
for their comforts, we must all allow."[15]

Anne Elliot, the middle daughter, was also connected to someone special in the navy. She had been engaged to Captain Frederick Wentworth, "a remarkably fine young man, with a great deal
of intelligence, spirit, and brilliancy"[16] but with, at that time, no
money, no connections, and no ship. In addition to her father's
disapproval, Lady Russell, who had been her late mother's best
friend and was like a surrogate mother herself, agreed with him:

> Anne Elliot, with all her claims of birth, beauty, and mind, to
> throw herself away at nineteen; involve herself at nineteen in an
> engagement with a young man, who had nothing but himself to
> recommend him, and no hopes of attaining affluence, but in the
> chances of a most uncertain profession, and no connexions to
> secure even his farther rise in that profession; would be, indeed,
> a throwing away, which she grieved to think of! Anne Elliot, so
> young; known to so few, to be snatched off by a stranger with-
> out alliance or fortune; or rather sunk by him into a state of
> most wearing, anxious, youth-killing dependance! It must not

be, if by any fair interference of friendship, any representations from one who had almost a mother's love, and mother's rights, it would be prevented.[17]

Thus Anne was persuaded by Lady Russell to break off the engagement to low-born, unconnected, and penniless Frederick Wentworth. Captain Frederick Wentworth then comes back into Anne's orbit after procuring—based on his own hard work and merit—a fortune in the navy with his own ship. Anne feels guilty and hopeless for not following her true inclinations when she first met him.

Even though Anne comes from an aristocratic family, she eschews the privilege and entitlement of her father and sisters. She is embarrassed by Sir Walter's "vacuity, Elizabeth's conceit, Mary's carping, and Lady Russell's 'prejudices on the side of ancestry.'"[18] Unlike the rest of her family and Lady Russell, Anne much prefers to live a life based on hard work and merit and seeks out others who prefer the same.

While "she was only Anne,"[19] the quiet, overlooked sister who fades into the background and isn't worth much to anyone but Lady Russell, she is also the hardest working, diligent, and capable one in her family; and this includes her unique capacity to care for other people. Anne is the one who packs up Kellynch Hall when they are forced to move. It is Anne who stays behind to tend to her nephew Walter when he is ill. It is Anne who cares for Louisa Musgrove when she experiences a serious fall and is concussed. Moreover, Anne stands up for those who have no one else to stand for them. In a confrontation with her father, she chooses a powerless, penniless dear friend over their aristocratic viscountess cousin.

The old school friend, Mrs. Smith, had been very kind to Anne when her mother died; Anne tries repay the kindness as

Mrs. Smith was a poor sickly widow, who had fallen on very hard times. Sir Walter is furious and incredulous that Anne would prefer visiting her lowly friend when they were invited to call upon his aristocratic cousin the Viscountess Lady Dalrymple. Her quiet rebellion makes him fume:

> A widow Mrs. Smith, lodging in Westgate-buildings!—A poor widow barely able to live, between thirty and forty—a mere Mrs. Smith, an every day Mrs. Smith, of all people and all names in the world, to be the chosen friend of Miss Anne Elliot, and to be preferred by her, to her own family connections among the nobility of England and Ireland! Mrs. Smith, such a name![20]

It is interesting that Jane Austen names this character who represents the opposite of privilege and entitlement "Smith." Smith is a common, generic name that reminds the internally referenced leader that last names don't matter. It doesn't matter who your parents are, what schools you attended, how much money your family has, or whatever other privileged club you may belong to. Mrs. Smith also reminds the internally referenced leader that value and worthiness are not connected to names and titles and connections. Rather, for the internally referenced leader, value comes from talent, hard work, and unselfish devotion to something greater than herself.

While the United States is famous for an American dream associated with rugged individualism and hard work, psychologists Jean M. Twenge and Keith Campbell claim that "the United States is currently suffering from an epidemic of narcissism."[21] Similarly, Harvard-trained moral philosophy professor at UC Irvine Aaron James has developed a theory that emanated from his concern "about the profusion of assholes in society and the serious possibility that the United States had already or almost become an 'asshole capitalist' system."[22] He defines asshole as "the guy (they are mainly men) who systematically allows himself advantages in social relationships out of an entrenched (and mistaken) sense of entitlement that immunizes him against the complaints of other people."[23] James describes the ways in which these systems of entitlement and privilege are "inherently prone to decline," especially as the community at large becomes fed up with unfair, unequal, and substandard treatment.[24] For example, the MeToo and Black Lives Matter movements reflect this upending of entrenched and oppressive paradigms.

In stark contrast to organizations based on entitlement and privilege, internally referenced leaders prefer systemic and explicit fairness. They strive to create and take part in organizations that utilize an objective and transparent system to hire, evaluate, promote, and reward their employees. Researchers have found that at many organizations, "women must perform at a higher standard than men to achieve the same level of success. This performance tax limits women's pay and promotion opportunities."[25] Thus, women thrive in cultures that explicitly value and reward hard work and merit rather than back channel relationships and cronyism. For example, in their book, *Through the Labyrinth: The Truth about How Women Become Leaders*, Alice Eagly and Linda Carli contend that it is much more conducive for women to become leaders and much better for organizations when there are objective fair performance evaluations and recruitment[26] rather than following the old boys' club. It's very important for promotions to be based on explicit, valid performance evaluations that "limit the influence of decision-makers' conscious and unconscious biases. . . . Without objective evaluations and open recruiting, biases very likely contaminate personnel decisions."[27] And there is the social psychology principle that like attracts like and people tend to use in-group loyalty to prefer and to interact with people like them.

The internally referenced leader uses clear rubrics that state explicit, objective, operationalized criteria, which have been agreed upon by multiple stakeholders in advance and which are applied consistently to everyone. Moreover, these criteria are directly related to job descriptions, job expectations, and job performance reviews. The internally referenced leader creates an organization that is fair, objective, and transparent, where everyone has an opportunity to succeed and where success is based on one's merits and hard work and not on taking shortcuts related to whom someone knows or how "special" that person might be.

The desire for a shortcut doesn't always come from having an inflated view of ourselves. It sometimes is the result of deepseated insecurity and a sense of unworthiness. Perhaps even those who perceive themselves as special, like Sir Walter Elliot, doubt themselves underneath a façade of bravado. In *The Self-Esteem Trap: Raising Confident and Compassionate Kids in an Age of Self-Importance*, psychologist Polly Young-Eisendrath warns that "the trouble with being special is that it frequently leads to being trapped in negative self-absorption. Parents and children have been taught otherwise: that being and feeling special leads to happiness and positive self-regard. It is deeply and sadly ironic that it has almost the opposite effect."[28]

Internally referenced leaders don't need or take shortcuts no matter how enticing. They don't need to be taken care of or treated as special. That's always a trap. It often communicates an underlying message of unworthiness that they cannot do work themselves and achieve goals on their own merits. This is damaging to one's self-efficacy and self-esteem. Think of "Operation Varsity Blues," the California college cheating scandal. In 2019, more than fifty people were indicted in a college admissions bribery scandal that included thirty-three parents. They paid admissions consultant William Rick Singer millions of dollars to secure admission to elite universities. Students were recruited as athletes—even if they did not play the sport in question. Singer also helped them cheat on or have others take their standardized college exams.

Wharton business school professor of legal studies and business ethics Julian Jonker and USC professor of management Shaun Harper acknowledge, "In the first instance, the victims are the students who would have gotten places but for the scam. But really the next victim is public confidence. . . . What we as people in universities need to do is to really fight for this idea that what we reward is raw talent, perseverance, grit and character."[29]

But aren't the students whose parents cheated and broke the law by committing fraud to purchase their college admissions also victims? This audacious shortcut and inside fix got those kids kicked out of college to face public mortification, but even more grievous is what the deceitfulness probably did to them on the inside. It sent a message that they are unworthy and that the only way they can achieve success is if Mommy or Daddy buys it for them. This is done all the time, by the way, without breaking the law, and it is equally devastating to a young or old person's self-esteem. Even worse than helicopter parents, lawnmower parents mow down any difficult person or condition in order to prevent their child from experiencing struggle, failure, and ultimately growth. Life coach and parenting consultant Jacque Nelson describes it this way: "This misaligned parenting strategy is 'fearful loving,' where parents, in spite of good intentions, ironically end up hampering, disempowering, and sending the message that their children are not capable."[30] As self-esteem psychologist Polly Young-Eisendrath notes, "It's baffling when parents have no confidence in their children's ability to solve their own problems yet want them to become self-confident."[31] Once they arrive in the workplace, it is very difficult for these young people to become internally referenced when they have been externally coddled for so long.

No One So Capable as Anne

Those "sea-faring folks with weathered skin" think beyond their own individual self-interest. As an internally referenced leader, you, too, pursue collective thriving over individual comfort.

The educational leaders I've worked with in China exemplify what Robert Greenleaf calls Servant Leadership, in which the leader "begins with the natural feeling that one wants to serve, to serve first."[32] Jian Sun is president of WIA, an educational group affiliated with the prominent Chinese education organization CERNET, which runs several wraparound residential programs for Chinese students studying in the US. One of his campuses was not as ready as he would have liked it to be for the arrival of new students from China. Instead of getting angry or coming down on his staff, he literally rolled up his sleeves and asked to be assigned a manual work task. He was laughing as he showed me the scratches he got from getting rooms ready for these students.

I often bring the classic Chinese text by Lao Tzu, the *Tao Te Ching*, into my seminars and into my consulting and professional development with educational leaders in China. Like Austen's canon, it was very inspirational in the development of the theory of internally referenced leadership. Passage 17 reads this way: "When the master governs, the people are hardly aware that he exists. Next best is a leader who is loved. Next, one who is feared. The worst is one who is despised. / If you don't trust the people, you make them untrustworthy. / The Master doesn't talk, he acts. When his work is done, the people say, 'Amazing: we did it, all by ourselves!'"[33]

The *Tao Te Ching* celebrates the disappearing, humble leader who works for the collective good. It's not described only by Lao Tzu; it's also described by Austen in the person of Anne Elliot. Indeed, she is talked about as "Only Anne." Her vain, selfish, lazy father and sisters don't see her worthiness and don't see her hard work on behalf of others. But lots of other characters in her orbit notice not only how diligently and effectively she works but also how selfless she is. Anne is known for her industriousness, which stems from thinking of others before herself and thus acting for their well-being rather than her own. As David Shapard notes,

> It is remarkable that, after hearing news with such tremendous implications for herself, Anne's first conscious thoughts involve concern about the possibility of wrong behavior or suffering by others. In a letter to her niece about the novel, Jane Austen writes, "You may *perhaps* like the Heroine, as she is almost too good for me" (March 23, 1817).[34]

In Anne Elliot, Austen created a character who was too good for her and definitely too good for many of the people around her. Anne is someone who feels her duty and quietly acts on it. "Anne had every thing to do at once—the apothecary to send for—the father to have pursued and informed—the mother to support and keep from hysterics—the servants to control—the youngest child to banish, and the poor suffering one to attend and soothe":[35] "Anne's calm sensible actions in the face of an emergency."[36]

When Louisa Musgrove falls and experiences a nearly fatal concussion, it is quiet, selfless, but action-oriented Anne who steps in to care for her. Indeed, Captain Wentworth says with admiration, "But, if Anne will stay, no one so proper, so capable as Anne."[37] Anne's humble, take-charge authority is in stark contrast to the fecklessness of her family. Emily Auerbach talks about how "Austen underscores Anne's utility by contrasting it with other people's futility. Sir Walter finds the only 'occupation for an idle hour' to be reading about himself in the baronetage, and Elizabeth Elliot has 'no habits of utility.'[38] Neither of them thinks of other people, while Anne is always thinking of other people—not just her family but everyone with whom she comes into contact.

While Anne appears to be motivated by a loving heart and genuine desire to serve, there is also a need for her to claim her worthiness in the context of a family that is so entitled, privileged, and selfish. As Emily Auerbach says,

> Austen demonstrates that one key difference between Mary and Anne is that Anne has escaped the curse of "the Elliot self-importance." . . . Mary, Elizabeth, and Sir Walter all feel *ill used* rather than *of use* because they arrogantly expect one-way devotion and service from those around them. . . .
>
> In contrast, Anne has enough humility and perspective to know that her family does not deserve its rank. . . . Austen challenges traditional notions of class, gender, and success.[39]

The internally referenced leader takes full advantage of whatever responsibility or position she has to be of use rather than to feel entitled.

Honourable Toils, Just Rewards:
Learning to Brook Being Happier Than I Deserve

"They might in fact have borne down a great deal more than they met with, for there was little to distress them beyond the want of graciousness and warmth."[40] As an internally referenced leader, while you do put the communal good first, you also believe in delayed gratification.

I often think of the beautiful passage describing Anne Elliot and Frederick Wentworth's reunion after so many years.

> There they exchanged again those feelings and those promises which had once before seemed to secure everything, but which had been followed by so many, many years of division and es-

trangement. There they returned again into the past, more exquisitely happy, perhaps, in their re-union, than when it had been first projected; more tender, more tried, more fixed in a knowledge of each other's character, truth, and attachment; more equal to act, more justified in acting.[41]

This passage perfectly captures the beauty of two weathered souls finding each other again, finding love again, and appreciating it that much more for having lost and grieved and struggled for so long. Austen mentions how their "maturity of mind"[42] provides them an appreciation for love, intimacy, devotion, and commitment that they did not have in their younger years. There is a sense that her (relatively) older characters have earned this reunion after many years of hard work and struggle.

Internally referenced leaders believe in delayed gratification, which (if properly balanced) can be very useful to organizations so that they can consider the wider and long-lasting impact of any decision and keep the end goal in mind. These leaders know how to stay focused and work hard to get to the finish line. Daniel Goleman explains that "cognitive control enables executives to pursue a goal despite distractions and setbacks."[43] Internally referenced leaders are able to "pit self-restraint against self-gratification ... [and] concentrate on the future goal."[44]

Internally referenced leaders understand that we can fully metabolize and appreciate a satisfying result often after experiencing a long, hard journey. This is often true in the world of Austen. Moreover, Austen suggests that happy outcomes are not guaranteed and are not always permanent. As a smart and savvy navy wife, Mrs. Croft says, "But I hate to hear you talking so, like a fine gentleman, and as if women were all fine ladies, instead of rational creatures. We none of us expect to be in smooth water all our days."[45] Similarly, the internally referenced leader is able to savor and be grateful for the hard-won special precious moment that may be fleeting. Austen reminds the internally referenced leader that no matter how hard she works and how much she provides her community, she is not entitled to a happy ending. It signifies a grace beyond a ledger or accounting. As Captain Wentworth reflects,

> "I have been used to the gratification of believing myself to earn every blessing that I enjoyed. I have valued myself on honourable toils and just rewards. Like other great men under reverses," he added with a smile. "I must endeavour to subdue my mind to my fortune. I must learn to brook being happier than I deserve."[46]

Persuasion is Jane Austen's last and most mature novel, in which she poignantly and poetically reflects on a well-earned reward after a period of toil. She seems to contemplate the delayed and satisfying gratification of the worthy.

According to Stuart Tave,

> Captain Wentworth knows rather too much too easily. He is a lucky man. But he has always been used to the gratification of believing himself to have earned every blessing he enjoys, valuing himself on honorable toils and just rewards. His toils assuredly have been honorable[,] and he and his profession, Anne sees, deserve their rewards, while her useless father is unworthy to hold what he has inherited. But Wentworth also realizes, by the end, and it is a sort of pain which is new to him, that in gaining Anne after so misvaluing her, and after missing the opportunity to act, he has been given more than he has earned.[47]

For Jane Austen and the internally referenced leader, it's not about working hard and doing the right thing to earn some guaranteed big prize at the end. Rather, it's about working hard and striving to be worthy and appreciative of every realized mini-goal in a state of grace, knowing we are never entitled and none of it is guaranteed.

Sandy Lerner, cofounder of Cisco Systems, expressed such appreciation when asked whether she felt resentful about the unfair circumstances in which she was fired from the company she founded. Sandy started Cisco Systems with her ex-husband, Leonard Bosack, in their living room when they were graduate students at Stanford. In those early years, the couple struggled financially to keep the business going. They mortgaged their home, maxed out their credit cards, and ended up hiring friends so that they could offer deferred salaries and stock options. After three years, they finally received the outside funding they desperately needed in order to fill the many orders that were coming in for their revolutionary technology product.

That funding came from Donald Valentine, a venture capitalist who founded Sequoia Capital and was often referred to as the "Grandfather of Silicon Valley." Valentine took advantage of Sandy and Len's lack of business experience and convinced them to have his lawyer draft their vesting agreement with him. This enabled Valentine to have Sandy fired when their personal and professional conflicts intensified. Len resigned in solidarity with Sandy. The two of them sold their stock shortly thereafter, which was then worth about $170 million. Today, the stock would be worth more than $500 billion. For Sandy, the experience wasn't about the financial implications. It was about the work and the impact. She describes her life as "bold" and appreciates both her successes and her struggles.[48] Sandy says that she appreciates the many successes and the many struggles and getting to the next place. She went on to found and ultimately sell the cosmetics company Urban Decay. She also started an organic farm. She works hard and appreciates all the opportunities she has had for reinvention and all that she was able to achieve.

Simon Sinek, bestselling author of *Leaders Eat Last*, explains, "It is not when things come easily that we appreciate them, but [it's] when we have to work hard for them or when they are hard to get that those things have greater value to us."[49] The internally referenced leader appreciates all of it and strives to be worthy of all of it—her hard work and accomplishments, her struggles and losses and learning, and the amazing gifts that come in unexpected, miraculous, magical ways. Sandy Lerner's recent philanthropic endeavor has been a major restoration of Chawton House, which was once owned by Jane Austen's brother, Edward Austen Knight. Sandy opened the house to the public as the Center for the Study of Early Women's Writing. She is a hardworking, internally referenced leader and Janeite, who admits that Austen is her "drug of choice," which probably resulted in her feeling as much success from her hard journey as from her hard-won achievements.

Ruth Bader Ginsburg on "How Dare You" Entitlement

Ruth Bader Ginsburg said that "Feminism . . . [is the] notion that we should each be free to develop our own talents, whatever they may be, and not be held back by artificial barriers—manmade barriers, certainly not heaven sent."[50] Like many of us, Jane Austen would have been impressed with the late Supreme Court Justice, who spent her life fighting for women (and all people) to be judged on their merit and worthiness rather than on the basis of their sex.

Speaking to her close friend Nina Totenberg, NPR's Supreme Court reporter, before a packed house at the Sundance Film Festival for the 2018 premiere of the documentary *RBG*, Justice Ginsburg described experiencing sexual harassment before sexual harassment was even a legal concept. In her words, "every woman of my vintage knows what sexual harassment is, although we didn't have a name for it." Long before she was on the Supreme Court or was cofounder of the Women's Rights Project at the

American Civil Liberties Union, she was an undergraduate at Cornell University. It was the early 1950s, and young Ruth Bader was seeking help from a chemistry instructor for an upcoming test. He ended up giving her a practice exam that was identical to the real exam. She understood he was trading the answers and a good grade for sexual favors. "I knew exactly what he wanted in return," she said. She added that she then "went to his office and said, 'How dare you? How dare you do this?' And that was the end of that."[51]

Without any extra help and in spite of sexism, Ruth graduated first in her class at Cornell in 1954 with a degree in government. She then married Martin Ginsburg, a law student at Harvard. Their first year of marriage was challenging as they welcomed their first child and Marty was drafted into the military. After his discharge, the couple went back to Cambridge where they both enrolled at Harvard Law School. Ruth was one of only eight women in a class of five hundred. From the very beginning, she and the other few women faced a misogynistic environment, explicitly having to defend their presence to a dean who, at a welcome dinner that was anything but, asked them why they were taking prized spots away from men.

Undaunted by Harvard Law School or any other hostile environment, Ruth excelled academically and was the first woman admitted to the prestigious *Harvard Law Review* journal. While she worked hard at her studies as well as trying to be a caring young mother and wife, her everyday challenges were only exacerbated when Marty developed testicular cancer. Ruth must have been scared out of her mind, as she had lost her mother to cancer days before her own high school graduation. But Ginsburg was never a victim; she got to work. In addition to seeing to the health needs of her husband and taking care of their young daughter, Ruth not only attended her own classes but also went to take notes in Marty's classes. When Marty graduated and received a legal job in New York, Ruth transferred to Columbia Law School so they could be together. Of course, she excelled at Columbia, where she was elected to the *Columbia Law Review* journal and graduated first in her class. In spite of all the grinding years of hard work and merit, though, she was not able to get a job after law school because of the pervasive bias against hiring women in the legal profession. Not to be deterred, this inequity became the raison d'être of her professional life.

As a law professor at Rutgers and later as director of the Women's Rights Project of the American Civil Liberties Union, Ginsburg spent her life and career trying to educate entitled men (whether chemistry instructors or entire institutions) to view women based on their hard work and merit rather than their sex. At the ACLU, she argued six landmark cases before the US Supreme Court on gender equality. In 1980, President Carter appointed her to the US Court of Appeals; and in 1994, President Clinton nominated her to the US Supreme Court.

Writing for the majority in the landmark case of *United States v. Virginia*, Supreme Court Justice Ginsburg eloquently expressed the importance of recognizing women for their hard work and merit. The Virginia Military Institute (VMI) was the sole single-sex public college in Virginia. VMI stated its distinctive mission is to produce "'citizen soldiers,' men prepared for leadership in civilian life and military service." The United States sued Virginia and VMI alleging that VMI's exclusive male-only admission policy violated the Equal Protection Clause of the Constitution. In her decision holding that the male-only prohibition was unconstitutional, Justice Ginsburg wrote,

> [T]he Court has repeatedly recognized that neither federal nor state government acts compatibly with the equal protection principle when a law or official policy denies to women, simply because they are women, full citizenship stature—equal oppor-

tunity to aspire, achieve, participate in and contribute to society based on their individual talents and capacities.[52]

Feminist icons like Justice Ginsburg and Jane Austen grew up in a world of corsets of one kind or another and knew that the best way to truly burst out of them was to utilize their merit and capacity for hard work and insist that others do the same. Moreover, they also remind us to claim our hard work and take credit for our efficacy. As women, we often unwittingly participate in the paradigm of entitlement by deflecting and playing small so that others can take credit for our efforts and feel big.

How to Put More Anne in Your Life

For Anne Elliot, it is all about the satisfaction that comes from hard work. The most effective leaders are "sea-faring folks with weathered skin," who work hard for their success rather than having it handed to them. As an internally referenced leader, you prefer hard work and merit over privilege and entitlement. Those "sea-faring folks with weathered skin" think beyond their self-interest. As an internally referenced leader, you pursue collective thriving rather than selfish short-term interests. As an internally referenced leader, while you do put the communal good first, you also believe in delayed gratification of well-earned second chances and hard-won results. An internally referenced leader feels empowered and inspired when working with her own body, mind, and soul to achieve what she wants, which mostly is to make her world a better place.

Exercises for Operationalizing Principle 3

➤——————→

1. **Share Your Stretchmarks, War Wounds, and Kintsugi Pottery.**

Kintsugi is the Japanese art of repairing broken pottery by filling in the breaks with gold. Instead of hiding the breaks, they are showcased and celebrated as part of the vessel's history. What scars do you have, literally and figuratively? What do they signify you've been through? What did you learn? How did they help you grow? How are they beautiful in your life? Take a picture of them, and share with a trusted circle.

2. **Leave the Campground Better Than You Found It.**

How have you left the campground better than you found it? Keep a journal every day noting something you did to benefit others in your family, your friends, your organization, or your community, without credit or fanfare.

3. **Break Up with Your So-Called Saviors, Shortcuts, and Status.**

Think of a conflict that is either professional or personal. On some deep level, are you wishing or hoping or demanding that a shortcut, change in status, or savior riding in on a white horse will save the day and save you? Write any so-called saviors a breakup letter. Thank them for being part of the old paradigm; but tell them you will be fine, and they can ride their white horse somewhere else. You are an internally referenced leader who can handle anything that comes your way from a place of power based on your own hard work, merit, and worthiness.

4. Write Vows to Be Worthy of Your Gratifying Moments.

What gratifying moments have you experienced lately? What does it mean for your life? How does it make you feel? What part did you earn, and what part was grace? What vows can you make to be worthy of your goal from a space of appreciation and love?

4

A Better Guide in Ourselves

Like Fanny Price of *Mansfield Park*, insist on
faithfully following your internal moral compass and
normative principles, even in the face of external
pressure, coercion, and material consequence.

Meet Fanny Price

We meet Fanny Price at ten years old, living in an impoverished, chaotic home in Portsmouth with an unemployed, disabled, alcoholic father and a pregnant mother, who is about to have her ninth child. Her mother married significantly below her original station, while her aunt married in the opposite direction, as her spouse is Sir Thomas Bertram of the great estate of Mansfield Park in Northamptonshire.

After years of hardly any contact between the sisters, Fanny's destitute mother is forced to reach out to her older sister for financial support. In addition to offering money, Lady Bertram and Sir Thomas offer to have Fanny come live with them and their own children at Mansfield Park. As a timid young girl, Fanny finds herself lonely and demeaned at the great house. Fanny's other aunt, Mrs. Norris, treats her more like a servant than a niece, reminding her daily that she is "not a *Miss Bertram*."[1] While most of the Bertram family is dismissive, her cousin Edmund tries to be warm and kind, and they form a close connection that lasts from childhood into early adulthood.

When Fanny is eighteen, Sir Thomas and his eldest son, Tom, travel to Antigua to visit Sir Thomas's plantation, which is experiencing financial difficulty. Fanny is the only one who confronts Sir Thomas about engaging in the "slave trade," while the others say nothing in "dead silence."[2] Fanny, however, is a woman who is "firm as a rock in her own principles"[3] and, therefore, is unafraid to take a moral stand no matter how relatively introverted or powerless she might appear.

Fanny uses her internal "better guide"[4] to object to all kinds of morally dubious actions throughout the novel—especially when brother and sister Henry and Mary Crawford arrive at Mansfield Park. Henry is a handsome, selfish scoundrel who shamelessly seduces Fanny's engaged cousin Maria for sport. In addition to being repulsed by Henry, Fanny is also put off by his sister Mary, who uses her manipulative, condescending charm to flirt with Edmund and then demean him for choosing to be a clergyman. Admittedly to herself, Fanny is also jealous of Mary as she is starting to have romantic feelings for Edmund.

Things become even more complicated when Henry starts pursuing Fanny for his own amusement. He surprises himself, however, when he starts to actually fall in love with her, enchanted by her genuine and unflinching character and goodness. Fanny views Henry's behavior toward Maria as deplorable and does not return his feelings. He attempts to win her heart by securing a military promotion for her brother. He then proposes to Fanny and is shocked and devastated when she refuses. Sir Thomas is furious at Fanny's rejection of Henry because he sees it as an extremely advantageous match given Henry's eligibility and Fanny's low position. Sir Thomas threatens to banish Fanny from Mansfield Park and send her home to Portsmouth if she does not reconsider. Fanny responds vehemently, "Oh! never, never, never! He never will succeed with me."[5]

Unafraid to face the consequences of her stance, Fanny refuses Henry and returns to Portsmouth and finds her home to be "the abode of noise, disorder, and impropriety"[6] with a drunken, rough, coarse father and an overwhelmed mother, who prefers her sons over her daughters. She receives no attention from either of them, even though it had been over eight years since she was sent away. Fanny misses Mansfield Park for so many reasons, and the people of Mansfield Park equally miss Fanny and especially her good moral sense.

Henry Crawford runs away with her now-married cousin Maria, which results in a devastating scandal that humiliates the family in all the newspapers. Mary Crawford's selfish reaction to this incident as well as her disdain for Edmund's lack of inheritance causes her to break up with Edmund. When Edmund's brother Tom becomes seriously ill, Fanny is called back to Mansfield Park, where Sir Thomas apologizes for his cruelty and Edmund finds that he missed Fanny's loving presence and moral steadfastness. Edmund eventually realizes that he loves Fanny as much as she loves him, making Fanny very "happy in spite of every thing."[7]

If We Would Attend to It

"We have all a better guide in ourselves, if we would attend to it."[8] As an internally referenced leader, your starting point is this important leadership question: *What are my ethics and my responsibilities for living a worthy life for me?*

Like Fanny Price, Sharon Chuter has always known her moral

center and not been afraid to act from it. Raised in Nigeria, she didn't allow her desire for success and career trajectory to obfuscate her personal morals and, in fact, views her ethicality as a key to her professional and personal success. It did not preclude her speaking truth to power even then. She says, "For me, one of the most common themes in my life is always standing up for what I believe is right and always fighting for a better world, you know, from being expelled when I was in high school for mobilizing everyone to go on strike."[9] Sharon says that it "took that craziness of a teenager not knowing how to take *no* for an answer" to bulldoze her way into a job at Revlon.[10] True to form, she won them over by challenging Revlon on the fact that she could not get their makeup products in Nigeria and that most of their product line was Anglocentric. She ended up getting the job and getting Revlon into Nigeria as well as other African countries and helping them diversify their shade range and staff.

In spite of these accomplishments, Sharon did not feel that her ethical values to create a truly diverse cosmetics company were being fully realized. She cited the fact that the biggest skin products in Africa were still skin bleachers, which were injurious to both physical and mental health. Therefore, Sharon formed her own company called UOMA in order to create "the most inclusive black-owned beauty brand" and "to re-write the rules of inclusivity and diversity to create a world of beauty that truly is for all of us."[11] In creating makeup for everyone, UOMA offers fifty-one shades and is sold in major retail outlets around the world as well as on its website.

In spite of UOMA's success, Sharon's moral mandate was still not satisfied. In the wake of the murders of George Floyd, Breonna Taylor, and the many other black victims of horrific racism, she wanted to hold corporate America accountable for its hypocrisy:

The trigger for me was seeing all these brands post for George Floyd and blacking out their Instagram on Tuesday. . . . And I just thought, why are you absolving yourselves of the role you've played in creating this problem? How are you not seeing the connection between your depriving people of color of economic opportunities and the oppression?

Let's stop talking about it. Talk is cheap. You can't say Black lives matter if you don't have any Black employees in your office.[12]

Sharon noted that it was hypocritical for these corporations to express solidarity with the Black Lives Matter movement when 8 percent of the people employed in white-collar professions are black and only 3.2 percent of those are in senior management positions. In response, Sharon started the "Pull Up or Shut Up" campaign, which asks companies to release the total number of black executives at their companies. For Chuter, an individual and corporate ethical stance must be in both word and deed.

In their *Harvard Business Review* article entitled "How to Design an Ethical Organization," Nicholas Epley of the University of Chicago Booth School of Business and Amit Kumar of the University of Texas address the importance for leaders to articulate in advance both personal and organizational ethics. Through their research, they have found that ethical leadership creates and is supported by an ethical culture. It is absolutely critical that "strategies and practices . . . be anchored to clearly stated principles that can be widely shared within the organization."[13] They explain that articulating these values in advance is key to encouraging and ensuring ethical behavior: "Most people have less difficulty knowing what's right or wrong than they do keeping ethical considerations top of mind when making decisions. Ethical lapses can therefore be reduced in a culture where ethics are at the center of attention."[14]

An internally referenced leader tries to identify her moral line in advance and be willing to enforce it to the extent she can. These scrupulous role models remind me of Fanny Price from *Mansfield Park*, who always honored her internal better guide—her internal moral line. Fanny's virtuous sensibility was fixed; it never wavered, no matter what the cost. Fanny paid a price for standing her ground. Perhaps that is why she is considered somewhat of a prude compared to other Austen heroines.

Fanny Price is not one of the favorites in the Jane Austen canon. As iconic literary critic Lionel Trilling famously noted,

> there is one novel of Jane Austen's, *Mansfield Park*, in which the characteristic irony seems not to be at work. Indeed, one might say of this novel that it undertakes to discredit irony and to affirm literalness, that it demonstrates that there are no two ways about anything. And *Mansfield Park* is for this reason held by many to be the novel that is least representative of Jane Austen's peculiar attractiveness, . . .
>
> And they can point to *Mansfield Park* to show what the social coercion is in all its literal truth, before irony has beglamoured us about it and induced us to be comfortable with it. . . . No other great novel has so anxiously asserted the need to find security, to establish, in fixity and enclosure, a refuge from the dangers of openness and chance.[15]

Trilling talks about "fixity" and "enclosure" and "security" with respect to Fanny Price. Fanny has less security or certainty than any of the other Austen heroines. At ten years old she trades her destitute parents, including an alcoholic father, for a wealthy aunt and uncle who ignore her most days and treat her like a second-class poor relation on good days. Meanwhile, her Aunt Norris is explicitly condescending to poor Fanny. In all the years she lives there, Fanny's residency is never secure. She is never made to feel truly at home at Mansfield Park; she never really belongs. Indeed, her uncle displaces her in dramatic fashion when he cruelly sends her back home into poverty because she refuses to marry the morally bankrupt Henry Crawford. Moreover, she does not belong back at home with her parents either. She is an outsider in both places.

Thus, the only real fixity and security in Fanny's life is her unwavering moral center. It is the only place where she feels truly at home. Austen describes Fanny as "the only one who has judged rightly throughout, who has been consistent . . . from first to last." She is described as relatively small, feeble, uneducated, and powerless when compared to her more robust and dominant relations, and yet her "exacting moral standards"[16] separate her from everyone in her surroundings and in some ways make her the most powerful of all. According to Stuart Tave, "[i]t is always Fanny who sees the entire process, who sees what others are doing when they themselves do not understand their own actions, sees the whole drama of their interaction. Her propriety has a large source and is a comprehensive virtue."[17]

In the spirit of Fanny Price, the internally referenced leader has a clear, unwavering internal moral compass that governs her perspective and behavior as much as possible. Iconic management author and educator Peter Drucker, who has been described as the "founder of modern management,"[18] calls this the "Mirror Test,"[19] where the most important questions are always these: *What are my values* and *does my behavior comport with the values of the person in the mirror in every situation*?

Not everyone with strong values and a fixed center has the opportunity (some might say luxury) of leaving her job when she feels that her morals are compromised. Still, one can act on them in important ways even while staying in place. Take, for example, Heather. Her unexpected rise at the Lexus dealership provides an example of standing for one's moral ground while also staying in place.

Heather started working in the car industry more than fifteen years ago, while in her twenties. She says the "frat boy culture" made her want to quit, but she couldn't. She had rent, student loans, and family members to support, and the commission she earned from selling cars was "too hard to walk away from." For years, Heather says she put up with fellow sales associates who would be "demeaning" to her and "shockingly" even toward the female clients. When she was training, she had to "hide the nausea" because they would do anything they could to make a sale—no matter how uncomfortable they made the customer or how far they stretched the truth.[20] She worked with them but absolutely refused to become one of them.

Heather recalls meeting a single mother, who had been looking at a car. Given the woman's financial obligations, Heather urged her to think about a less expensive car, such as a Toyota. The woman thanked Heather and walked out. One of her fellow sales associates berated her for "not closing at any cost." Heather listened politely but was unmoved; she refused to become like him. After a few years, the transparency, dignity, and empathy with which Heather treated clients started to get the attention of the owners of the dealership. They promoted her to customer relations manager, where she focused on improving the customer experience by changing policies and procedures based on customer surveys and feedback. Heather urged the company to change its sales culture. Those who refused to comply with the new way of doing business were ultimately asked to leave. Heather's interventions were so effective that she was promoted again to her current position as new car sales manager, where she leads a team of almost all women. It took years, but all the salespeople on that floor now know that the most important thing to Heather—

and the company—is that they act with moral integrity in everything they do.

Conduct as the Result of Good Principles

"I speak of . . . conduct [as] the result of good principles."[21] As an internally referenced leader, your outward conduct aligns with your internal ethical principles.

The importance of ensuring that moral values align with action, whatever the cost, is integral to Robert Iger's leadership philosophy. Iger, the former CEO of Disney and its current executive chairman, believes there is "no price on integrity."[22] In his inspiring memoir and leadership treatise, *The Ride of a Lifetime: Lessons Learned from 15 Years as CEO of the Walt Disney Company*, he describes a particularly difficult moral dilemma involving television star Roseanne Barr. Barr and the original cast of *Roseanne* returned to ABC in 2017 to critical claim and very high ratings. Part of the appeal to ABC and to viewers was the way in which it reflected "a range of political reactions to the controversial subjects of the day."[23]

In May 2018, Barr wrote a deplorable and racist tweet about Valerie Jarrett, an esteemed senior advisor to former president Barack Obama. Iger knew the values of Disney needed to be reflected in its actions and not just its words. He asked his senior advisors about what the choices were. Among the options were suspension, loss of pay, and public rebuke. None of those consequences seemed severe enough to him, given the moral abhorrence of her actions. Iger wrote that he told executives then, "We don't have a choice here. . . . We have to do what's right. Not what's politically correct, and not what's commercially correct. . . . If any of our employees tweeted what she tweeted, they'd be immediately terminated."[24] Iger fired Barr that day, canceling her highly rated television program. He made it clear that "there's nothing more important than the quality and integrity of your people and your product. Everything depends on upholding that principle."[25]

Internally referenced leaders do not just talk about their values; they act on them. Austen suggests that Fanny doesn't just feel her morals, she lives by them. David Shapard has said that Fanny's "strict standards" stem from her "emotional sensitivity."[26] Austen calls out clergy who don't practice what they preach, which contrasts greatly with Fanny Price who always does. In conversation with Miss Crawford, Edmund says,

> The *manners* I speak of, might rather be called *conduct*, perhaps, the result of good principles; the effect, in short, of those doctrines which it is their duty to teach and recommend; and it will, I believe, be everywhere found, that as the clergy are, or are not what they ought to be, so are the rest of the nation.[27]

For internally referenced leaders reminiscent of Fanny, it's not just about acting in accordance with morals for the sake of adhering to them; it's about feeling the need to be moral as a personal mission.

Henry Crawford, who had been living an extremely amoral life, is at first amused by Fanny's virtuousness in word and deed. Because she is so consistent, firm, and fixed in living her values and he cannot quite believe she is real, his amusement turns into awe. This is how Jane Austen describes his view of her:

> It was a picture which Henry Crawford had moral taste enough to value. Fanny's attractions increased—increased two-fold— for the sensibility which beautified her complexion and illumined her countenance, was an attraction in itself. He was no longer in doubt of the capabilities of her heart. She had feeling,

genuine feeling. It would be something to be loved by such a girl, to excite the first ardours of her young, unsophisticated mind! She interested him more than he had foreseen.[28]

"Unsophisticated mind" is a compliment in Henry's view because the morality coming from her heart is pure and strong and has not yet been corrupted by the outside world. He erroneously assumes that because she is the naïve, quiet, poor cousin, she has retained some kind of innocence, which is the reason she is so kind and good. I would beg to differ, however. At a very young age, Fanny was exposed to extreme poverty, alcoholism, and abuse. She is wise to the traumas of the world and yet retains an internal moral compass that is pristine and unaffected by the often-cruel outside world. That's exactly what makes this seemingly quiet, poor, and disenfranchised young woman so powerful.

A Woman Who Is Firm as a Rock

"A woman, who [is] firm as a rock in her own principles"[29] acts in spite of consequence. As an internally referenced leader, you act in accordance with your internal ethics despite the external pressure or consequences.

What does it take for the powerless to stand up to the powerful, even at great personal cost and in spite of extreme external coercion? I wondered this in September 2018 as I listened to Dr. Christine Blasey Ford testify under oath before the Senate Judiciary Committee regarding the nomination of Brett Kavanaugh to the US Supreme Court.

After establishing her educational and professional credentials, Dr. Ford, whose voice was noticeably shaking, said,

I am here today not because I want to be. I am terrified. I am here because I believe it is my civic duty to tell you what happened to me while Brett Kavanaugh and I were in high school. I have described the events publicly before. I summarized them in my letter to Ranking Member Feinstein, and again in my letter to Chairman Grassley. I understand and appreciate the importance of your hearing from me directly about what happened to me and the impact it has had on my life and on my family.[30]

Dr. Ford went on to describe in great detail how she was sexually assaulted by Kavanaugh when they were both in high school. She closes her statement describing the impact of this testimony on her and her family.

Since September 16, my family and I have been living in various secure locales, with guards. This past Tuesday evening, my work email account was hacked and messages were sent out supposedly recanting my description of the sexual assault.

Apart from the assault itself, these last couple of weeks have been the hardest of my life. I have had to relive my trauma in front of the entire world, and have seen my life picked apart by people on television, in the media, and in this body who have never met me or spoken with me. I have been accused of acting out of partisan political motives. Those who say that do not know me. I am a fiercely independent person and I am no one's pawn. My motivation in coming forward was to provide the facts about how Mr. Kavanaugh's actions have damaged my life, so that you can take that into serious consideration as you make your decision about how to proceed. It is not my responsibility to determine whether Mr. Kavanaugh deserves to sit on the Supreme Court. My responsibility is to tell the truth.[31]

Dr. Ford and others who speak truth to power in such a public and personally vulnerable context for the greater good display what Harvard psychologist Howard Gardner calls "the Ethical Mind."[32] In the *Harvard Business Review*, Dr. Gardner describes the particular ethical mind of the whistleblower who steps back from personal and self-interested concerns and considers the nature of work and the community in a larger way, so that her "own momentary well-being is less important than the broader mission."[33] The internally referenced leader strives to have this broader mission for the good of the organization and the good of society by acting on those high moral values in all aspects of her life. She may also need to be willing to suffer the consequences even when the cost is very high.

Fanny Price spoke truth to power and suffered the consequences. Of all the heroines in Jane Austen's creation, Fanny had the least power of all. She had the least money. She had the fewest number of friends. Austen, however, says she was a woman who was "firm as a rock in her own principles"; and that enabled her to stand up to the most powerful of all, Sir Thomas Bertram, even though she was forced to suffer severe consequences, including banishment to her impoverished, alcohol-ridden destructive home.

As Rachel Brownstein says, in many ways *Mansfield Park* is "the story of Fanny Price and her much grander uncle[,] Sir Thomas Bertram (who admires her figure and also cruelly tries to give her to that unexpected high bidder, Henry Crawford)."[34] David Shapard adds that by defying her uncle's wishes in refusing to marry morally dubious Henry, "she does reveal in response to Henry's proposal a firmness that surprises everyone[;] . . . her moral principles tell her to stand firm and resist, since she is being asked to marry a man she considers morally defective."[35] Risking and receiving her uncle's wrath and banishment based on her morally driven behavior causes her undue hardship and suffering. As Stuart Tave describes, this as a "severe and revealing test"[36] when Sir Thomas Bertram sends her back to live in squalor with her impoverished family as a consequence.

Sir Thomas's punishment of Fanny for standing up for her

moral beliefs may also reflect a deeper amorality. Scholars have suggested that the deep moral concerns with Sir Thomas also reflect Austen's deep moral concerns with slavery. Indeed, quiet Fanny is the only character who dares confront Sir Thomas about his involvement in the insidious slave trade, as she mentions to her cousin Edmund, "Did not you hear me ask him about the slave-trade last night?"[37] Among the scholars who have discussed the connection between *Mansfield Park* and the slave trade is Helena Kelly. Pointing out that Austen appears to have named the novel after Lord Mansfield, who outlawed slavery in England, Kelly offers her justification of that assumption:

> It would have been unforgivably careless of Jane to attach Mansfield's name, out of all the names she could have chosen, to *this* novel unless she meant her readers to think about him and about slavery. There are brief references to the slave trade in *Emma* and to property in the West Indies in *Persuasion*. But in *Mansfield Park* two characters—the forbidding Sir Thomas Bertram and his eldest son, Tom—actually travel abroad to the Caribbean. And they go, Jane tells us specifically, to oversee the management of their estate in the sugar island of Antigua. . . .
>
> But what did Jane herself think? We know that she read Thomas Clarkson's *History of the Abolition of the Slave-Trade*, detailing his experiences over decades of campaigning against slavery. She even describes herself as having been "in love" with Clarkson—a love that tells us far more about her than her feelings for any of her supposed suitors do.
>
> She paid Clarkson a peculiar compliment. Mrs. Norris—Fanny's vicious bullying aunt—shares her name with a real-life slave trader and anti-abolitionist: Mr. Norris of Liverpool, the man Clarkson cast as chief villain in his book.[38]

Fanny stands for the proposition that no one should be sold or owned by anyone else, no matter how rich and no matter how powerful. For me and my leadership practice, she also represents how the internally referenced leader does not sell out her ideals. In describing Jane Austen's specific antislavery, abolitionist interest and references in *Mansfield Park*, Rachel Cohen considers how Austen is also speaking about the broader themes of freedom and power writ large:

> In the novel, Mansfield Park is called a "plantation," suggesting a similarity or an interconnectedness but not, I think, an equivalence. Jane Austen carefully did not write that the life led by enslaved persons was in any way equivalent to the life led by her characters. . . . Rather, the shared Mansfield name makes a kind of locus of overlaps where you have to think about history and power, where you must reckon with kinds of restriction.[39]

The power dynamic and history of oppression in *Mansfield Park*, however, is not as static and fixed as it may appear; and through the course of the novel, Fanny's moral imperative seems to transcend any physical restriction. As Stuart Tave observes, "Fanny the poor dependent, on whom so many try to impose themselves, takes upon herself the direction of no one; . . . but [she] becomes an important influence on the lives of so many of those who try to direct her and then find themselves dependent on her."[40] Sir Thomas and the others in her orbit learn and grow based on Fanny's great act of moral courage.

Austen also comments on Fanny's happy ending and self-contentment, given all that she has endured:

> Let other pens dwell on guilt and misery. I quit such odious subjects as soon as I can, impatient to restore every body, not greatly in fault themselves, to tolerable comfort, and to have done with all the rest.
>
> My Fanny indeed at this very time, I have the satisfaction of knowing, must have been happy in spite of every thing.[41]

Scholars have noted that it's very rare for Jane Austen to talk about her heroines so personally in the novel as she does when she writes, "My Fanny." As David Shapard states, "while always evincing sympathy for her heroines, the author never otherwise refers to one in so intimate a manner. This may reflect an almost maternal tenderness for Fanny Price, due to her timidity and sensitivity and to the extensive tribulations she suffers over the course of the story."[42] I would argue with Shapard that "timidity and sensitivity" don't define her but rather that Fanny should be characterized by her internally referenced, unwavering moral courage.

How to Put More Fanny in Your Life

Like Fanny Price, insist on faithfully following your internal moral compass, even in the face of external pressure, coercion, and material consequence. As an internally referenced leader, your starting point is always asking yourself about your ethics and responsibilities for living a worthy life before you go into any situation. As an internally referenced leader, your outward conduct aligns with your internal ethical principles as much as possible without regard to the external pressure or repercussions.

Exercises for Operationalizing Principle 4

➵━━━━━▶

1. A) Recall the Last Time You Flunked the Mirror Test.

Write about the last time you flunked the Mirror Test. The Mirror Test, conceived by management guru Peter Drucker, requires us to ask ourselves every day, "What kind of person do I want to see in the mirror?"[1] Is the person looking back at me now the person I want to see? We all have moments when we ignore our "better [moral] guide" and do things that we regret later on. What was your experience? How and why were you out of alignment with your moral center? How did it make you feel?

B) Write a "Better Guide" Script.

If you could go back and rewrite that moment in your life, what would you do differently then to be an internally referenced leader in alignment with your moral guide? What would you say differently? How would you think about it differently? I call this internally referenced Soul Fiction—rewriting the scenario so you can learn from it and be in internally referenced alignment next time.

2. Create a Moral Catch Phrase.

The internally referenced leader often crafts a moral catch phrase that she can use to help make decisions and stay in alignment when situations get wobbly or potentially compromising. The catch phrase should be personal and meaningful to you. You can always draw on the tried and true: *Do No Harm*; *Everything to*

Help, Nothing to Hinder; *Love and Compassion for Self and Others*; *Do Unto Others As You Would Have Done to You*; *Hate Has No Home Here,* or something similar. Place a card somewhere near (your purse, backpack, wallet, etc.) that has your moral catch phrase on one side and a reminder image on the other. My moral catch phrase is *Act As If Your Kids Are in the Room*, and my image is a picture of me and my son, Josh, in front of the Holocaust Memorial in Berlin. I experienced anti-Semitism at a party once and felt awful that I did not have the courage to speak up. I wish I had had my card to remind me. I now take it everywhere I go to summon the Fanny Price bravery that is always within and always there when I need it.

3. Create a Paint-by-Numbers Profile in Courage.

Think of a person you know or have read about who has displayed extraordinary moral courage. This person stood up for what they believed at great personal risk, facing possible or actual serious consequences. Why do you admire this person? What attributes do they have that enabled them to display such courage? How can you cultivate these attributes in yourself? To make internally referenced leadership in this area more accessible, it's important to disaggregate this model of moral courage by enumerating each specific attribute that comprises the whole. For example, a student in one of my classes risked her own job to blow the whistle on her particular school for violations of the Individuals with Disabilities Education Act. When I talked about her and Fanny Price to another group of students, the students in the class were very impressed, but they couldn't fathom doing the same themselves. I asked them to parse and identify the components of what it took for her to be so brave and so bold. They came up with qualities that included caring about kids who need services, believing in social justice, and honoring the sacred role of educator. These were all attributes they saw in themselves or that they were cultivating in themselves. This made the role model's profile in courage much more accessible to them.

5

"Learning to Love Is the Thing"

Like Catherine Morland of *Northanger Abbey*, protect
and retain your internal childlike dreaming, wonder, curiosity,
passion, and hope—especially in an external world that can
be discouraging, disillusioning, and filled with despair.

Meet Catherine Morland

Catherine Morland is a seventeen-year-old young woman with a big heart, enthusiastic spirit, and propensity to get lost in romance novels. When her family's wealthy neighbors, Mr. and Mrs. Allen, ask her to spend the season in Bath with them, Catherine enters a wider world and eventually becomes the heroine of her own story. At her very first ball, she meets Henry Tilney, and while she does not quite understand his gentle sarcasm, he dazzles her with his intelligence, wit, and genuine warmth.

Henry is taken by Catherine's innocence and wonder at being in society. While she learns a lot from him at the ball, he also learns from her innocent nature. On their first walk through the woods, he finds himself looking at the world in a fresh way through her appreciative and present eyes. He is taken with her new "source[s] of enjoyment"[1] in every moment in Bath and with her affinity for all she encounters, claiming, "The mere habit of learning to love is the thing."[2]

Catherine widens her circle in Bath in other ways. She meets her brother James's Oxford classmate John Thorpe, who, erroneously believing that the childless Allens have made Catherine their heir, sets his designs on becoming engaged to her. His equally manipulative sister, Isabella, views herself as more worldly than Catherine and offers to teach her about sophisticated life in Bath. Like her brother, Isabella is misinformed about Catherine and her brother James's financial situation and tries to manipulate them to get a proposal from James.

Catherine much prefers spending time with Henry Tilney and his sister Eleanor. She also views them as more worldly and knowledgeable than herself, but, unlike the Thorpes, they do not take advantage of her pure, good nature. They celebrate Catherine's innocence, curiosity, and enthusiasm. Her unwavering optimism is baffling and elusive, especially given their tragedy in losing their mother to an early death and their subsequent life with a cold and emotionally abusive father.

Initially their father, General Tilney, expresses disapproval of Catherine. But when he hears the rumor that Catherine will inherit the Allens' estate, he becomes an eager supporter of the budding romance between Catherine and Henry. Henry and Eleanor are shocked and pleased when their curmudgeon of a father warmly invites Catherine to stay with them at Northanger Abbey. Henry and his sister Eleanor enjoy Catherine's awe while roaming the grounds at Northanger and her "pleasure of walking and breathing fresh air."[3]

The Gothic architecture of the great Northanger Abbey unleashes Catherine's fantasies, which have been shaped by the Gothic romance novels in which she often loses herself. She imaginatively weaves vague information about Henry's mother and father into a dark tale of confinement and murder. When Henry catches her searching his late mother's room for proof of her outlandish theory, he expresses profound disappointment. He informs her that his father did not kill his mother and, in fact, grieved when she died in spite of the sometimes cold and loveless way in which he treated her. Henry then must go away on curate business, and Catherine worries that she may have ruined their relationship for good.

While Henry is gone, General Tilney abruptly forces Catherine to leave Northanger in the early morning hours, traveling home all by herself in public transportation without any escort— which was very dangerous for a young woman at that time. Catherine assumes that the general found out about her outrageous view of him and justifiably banished her in humiliation. She is not bitter about how she was treated; she understands how angry General Tilney and Henry must have been with her. And she is full of love and gratitude when she finally reunites with her family after the long and arduous seventy-mile journey. No matter what Catherine endures, she is an optimist who remarks that "storms and sleeplessness are nothing when they are over."[4]

While Catherine enjoys being home, she cannot stop thinking about Henry and about how her love for him continues. She tries to put those notions behind her, refusing to read romance novels anymore. Then, while lingering outside in her family garden, Catherine is surprised to find Henry approaching on horseback. He feels terrible about how his father treated her and explains that the cruel banishment was due to his discovery that he was mistaken in his belief that she was the wealthy Allens' heir. Moreover, a bitter John Thorpe told the general that Catherine's family was destitute, which was also a lie. In an angry rage, General Tilney forbids Henry from marrying Catherine. Henry breaks from his father and pursues Catherine anyway. While she is elated, her parents urge them to get General Tilney's consent. He eventually acquiesces when he learns that, while the Morlands may not be extremely rich, they are far from destitute. And as far as Henry is concerned, Catherine is the most affluent bride in the universe.

The Mere Habit of Learning to Love Is the Thing

"The mere habit of learning to love is the thing"[5] that makes a dreaming, passionate nature more potent than naïve. As an internally referenced leader, you do not just use your right brain as refuge; it is also a rich inner resource.

Catherine Morland often gets a bad rap in Austen's canon as the immature, frivolous, romance-reading, lightweight heroine. Kathleen Anderson has called Catherine "naïve,"[6] "Austen's least intelligent heroine,"[7] and "Austen's . . . least . . . mature" heroine.[8] Moreover, she places her in a category she calls "feminist fools."[9] Given these attributes, it might seem as though Catherine wouldn't have the chops to be an inspiration, much less emblematic of internally referenced leadership. In some ways for me, however, she is the most important internally referenced heroine of all. I could not have accomplished anything significant in my professional or personal life, including writing this book, without the example and instruction of Catherine Morland.

Catherine reminds me to tap into my wonder, curiosity, passion, and hope every day, especially when things are challenging and difficult. Catherine's abilities have been invaluable to me, enabling me to energize, problem-solve, create, and manifest wonderful things in my life, as well as remain hopeful and positive when going through demanding and unanticipated life-changing experiences.

Catherine's naïveté is a kind of right-brain wisdom that's essential for internally referenced leaders. In describing Catherine, Henry Tilney says,

But now you love a hyacinth. So much the better. You have gained a new source of enjoyment, and it is well to have as many holds upon happiness as possible. Besides, a taste for flowers is always desirable in your sex, as a means of getting you out of doors, and tempting you to more frequent exercise than you would otherwise take. And though the love of a hyacinth may be rather domestic, who can tell, the sentiment once raised, but you may in time come to love a rose?

But I do not want any such pursuit to get me out of doors. The pleasure of walking and breathing fresh air is enough for me, and in fine weather I am out more than half my time.—Mamma says, I am never within.

At any rate, however, I am pleased that you have learnt to love a hyacinth. The mere habit of learning to love is the thing; and a teachableness of disposition in a young lady is a great blessing.—Has my sister a pleasant mode of instruction?[10]

The mere habit of learning to love is essential for the internally referenced leader. It could be loving the hyacinth or loving the stimulating project you're working on or even loving the mindless task that needs to be done.

Catherine cultivates that state of appreciation and openness irrespective of what she's doing—a genuine, "unaffected pleasure."[11] Thus, she brings that state to whatever task is at hand or wherever she finds herself; it is not situation dependent. She's strictly BYOJ—she brings her own joy wherever she goes.

Catherine does not just love life, but she loves *loving* life. She exudes wonder and enthusiasm in everything she does. She is described as possessing childlike innocence, but it is not an insult—quite the opposite. As Stuart Tave says, Catherine is happy and satisfied "because her 'expectations' had been . . . 'unfixed'."[12] She's open to possibility. She hasn't been domesticated; she hasn't been restrained.

That childlike wonder is the ultimate beginner's mind; therefore Catherine always brings a fresh perspective and always welcomes new experiences. As Emily Auerbach says, "although Catherine initially accepts Henry Tilney as the end-all of knowledge, Austen shows us that sometimes the pupil knows more than the teacher; the fool sees more than the king."[13]

Thus, with Catherine's passion, love, and unfixed, childlike eyes, she can see more and feel more without any preexisting filter. Auerbach further describes that "throughout *Northanger Abbey*, Catherine's remarks are refreshingly blunt. She has not acquired adult dishonesty, indirection, or guile. As Henry quips, 'your mind is warped by an innate principle of general integrity.'"[14] She is the one in the room who can see that the emperor has no clothes. She speaks honestly and openly, without adult self-consciousness or agenda. Even at the end of the novel as she becomes more worldly wise, her disposition has not changed; and she has not absorbed any of the cynicism or guile that she has observed from her surrounds.

That childlike wonder, openness, and honesty are absolutely needed in the adult workplace. In his seminal book, *Flow: The Psychology of Optimal Experience*, professor of psychology and management Mihaly Csikszentmihalyi describes his theory of Flow, in which he develops an intrinsically motivated, optimal state for creativity and effectiveness. When people are in flow, they are at their happiest and most engaged, so completely absorbed in the task at hand that they almost become one with it. Csikszentmihalyi explains that we can best understand flow by watching children because "the rapt concentration on the child's face as she learns each new skill is a good indication of what enjoyment is about."[15] Csikszentmihalyi laments that "Unfortunately, this natural connection between growth and enjoyment tends to disappear with time."[16] The flow state provides "a sense of discovery"[17] and a sense of play, but we need to tap into that Catherine Morland childlike exuberance in order to feel it.

According to Brigid Schulte, best-selling author of *Overwhelmed: Work, Love, and Play When No One Has the Time*, "mothers have given up time to play"; but most women have done the same.[18] Research shows that they afford themselves little time for leisure. Schulte tries to understand this phenomenon as she challenges herself and all women "to find time to do good work *and* splash in puddles" in order to enjoy what Erik Erikson called the "three great arenas: work, love, and play."[19]

Executive coach Rosamund Stone Zander is also in the serious business of helping people work hard and play hard. She urges them to "give way to their passion"[20] by tapping into their childlike wonder, creativity, and sense of possibility. She develops programs for corporations and government agencies, as well as workshops she has offered at the Aspen Institute, World Economic Forum, and other global venues. Along with Benjamin Zander, Rosamund authored the book *The Art of Possibility*, in which they urge leaders to be "in a posture of openness, with an unfettered imagination for what can be." They explain that "in the realm of possibility, we gain our knowledge by invention. We decide that the essence of a child is joy, and joy she is."[21]

Dr. Donna Kiel brings childlike play, joy, and possibility into everything she does. A leadership expert and faculty member, who founded and directs the Office of Innovative Professional Learning at DePaul University College of Education, she provides consultation, professional development, mentoring, and other services to businesses, schools, organizations, and individuals. Whatever project Donna takes on or problem she tackles, she brings an infectious sense of wonder, curiosity, and especially play so that all the participants are fully engaged.

Donna explains that she devised her approach by adapting

MIT professor Scot Osterweil's "Four Freedoms of Play"[22] for an adult professional development audience to achieve what she calls "maximum creative productivity." The "Four Freedoms of Play" include the Freedom to Experiment in an open-ended, intrinsically motivated way, the Freedom to Fail and try again, the Freedom of Persona to try on different perspectives, and the Freedom of Effort to engage or disengage.[23] Donna says that "these playful inner-directed experiences captivate the participants through meaningful interactive activities that tap into their innate sense of joy."[24]

According to Donna, joy is "both a prerequisite and byproduct" of play. Her mentor—life coach and best-selling author of *The Joy Diet*, Martha Beck—showed her how to help herself and others "tap into their joy reservoir, which is absolutely essential for organizational learning and personal growth." Donna reveals, however, that her "greatest teacher" is "the brilliant and wise twelve-month-old Charlie Sue," her granddaughter. For Donna, Charlie is the embodiment of play, joy, and productive creativity, as she "is always full of awe and wonder and possibility" and "is always firmly situated in the present moment."[25] Channeling her granddaughter, Donna helps others to look at issues with a fresh perspective and unlimited possibility, just as she practices herself. Internally referenced leaders want their employees to play in order for them to love doing their work and maximize their creative contributions to their organizations and stakeholders.

Brendan Boyle, partner at the design and consulting firm IDEO, teaches a course about the connection between play and design thinking entitled From Play to Innovation. In thinking about how different kinds of play can engender passion and creativity in the workplace, he explains that "Cooperative Play" can lead to exciting and generative communal brainstorming sessions. He uses "Risk-Taking Play" to reinforce the "philosophy that it's okay to fail quickly in order to succeed sooner." Employees need to feel free to try on new ideas and articulate their out-of-the-box thinking without fear. He likes "Constructive Play" to help employees think "with their hands" and build something tangible. "Exploratory Play" facilitates examining different solutions. Brendan is fond of "Storytelling Play" to help stakeholders "better understand" and "embrace solutions" by putting themselves in the center of narrative.[26] He believes that even more than the ideas themselves, play can unleash our enthusiasm for the activity at hand and for life itself.

Catherine Morland is instructive because she is a master at play. She knows how to love whatever she's doing no matter how insignificant or simple. The internally referenced leader—whether boss or employee—tries to tap into this childlike enthusiasm and bring it to all activities, big or small. Observing a child at a playground or Catherine Morland in a garden, one can see them bringing an unabashed enthusiasm to everything they encounter, be it a flower or a castle. Jane Austen captures this enthusiasm the first time Catherine sees the estate, "Northanger Abbey!—These were thrilling words, and wound up Catherine's feelings to the highest point of extasy.[27] Her grateful and gratified heart could hardly restrain its expressions within the language of tolerable calmness."[28] Stuart Tave says, "Her happiness comes easily and she is often a fool, but it would be churlish not to sympathize with that time of young happiness when life is always outdoing itself in promise."[29] Scholar Helena Kelly says, "She retains a tendency to run rather than walk."[30]

Being able to cultivate playful joy from the inside out like Catherine Morland is essential for the internally referenced leader and makes her particularly mindful. The *15 Commitments of Conscious Leadership* includes a commitment that (apart from the fact that she's a fictional young woman from the 1800s and not a twenty-first-century businesswoman) seems to describe Catherine Morland to a *T*. Specifically, it states,

> I commit to creating a life of play, improvisation, and laughter. I commit to seeing all of life unfold easefully and effortlessly. I commit to maximizing my energy by honoring rest, renewal, and rhythm.
>
> I [don't] commit to seeing my life as serious [requiring] hard work, effort, and struggle . . . [and] play and rest as distractions from effectiveness and efficiency.[31]

Leadership coaches Jim Dethmer, Diana Chapman, and Kaley Warner Klemp of the Conscious Leadership Group talk about the importance of creating a workday that is as joyful as possible. They suggest that "children and animals" are wonderful role models.[32] I would argue that Catherine Morland is also a role model for self-generated, joyous, conscious play. Internally referenced leaders don't take themselves too seriously; and they encourage others to experiment and trust without fear of failure or reprisal. In his *Harvard Business Review* article entitled "Making Joy a Priority at Work," Alex Liu, managing partner and chairman of global management consulting firm A. T. Kearney, emphasizes the importance of creating a culture of joy in one's organization. He explains what Catherine Morland innately knows to be elemental: "joy connects people more powerfully than almost any other human experience."[33]

A New Source of Enjoyment

"You have gained a new source of enjoyment."[34] As an internally referenced leader, your inner, childlike wonder encourages play and passion, helping you achieve greater creativity and flow.

That childlike sense of wonder and enjoyment can be used (and is sometimes required) to tackle some of the most difficult and seemingly intractable adult problems. It may seem counterintuitive, but the more serious and grown-up the problem, the more need for play—for risk taking, for out-of-the-box thinking, and for innovation. This was certainly the case for Kim Lloyd. Kim has been a police officer for over twenty years. She comes from and patrols an area of Chicago called Englewood, which is one of the most impoverished neighborhoods in the city and one that is desperately in need of resources and services. She considers Englewood home and says she is often "heartsick" at the "poverty, unemployment, crime, and institutional racism" she encounters on a regular basis and even in her own police department. Kim says she is limited as a police officer when she is called to respond to violent situations. For her, it is often "too little too late."[35]

In order to work on "root causes and prevention" of what she calls "so many babies who get caught up in the system," Kim enrolled in DePaul's doctoral program in educational leadership.[36] She is one of the most enthusiastic and exuberant students I have ever encountered. Many students struggle and ache in their quest for the "right" dissertation topic. Kim, however, reveled in the process of exploring the myriad research questions she wanted to ask. I had never seen a student so buoyant about such a rigorous endeavor.

At first, she was interested in addressing the school-to-prison pipeline. This topic transformed into African American boys' precipitous drop in grades in the fourth grade. She then looked at teacher-implicit bias and systemic racism in elementary schools. This morphed into an historical examination of the inequities in school law and policy. Finally, Kim told me that she landed on a lack of teacher preparedness in literacy. It seemed as though Kim was scattered—and I was worried she was overly ambitious. I asked her to meet with me in person to explain her trajectory.

I wanted to help her focus. But it was actually Kim who helped me. She taught me that her Catherine Morland–style exuberance and divergent thinking were integral to productive creativity. When Kim came to my office, she brought me a chart that left me speechless. It included a comprehensive diagram of all the factors impacting the education and welfare of African American boys, demonstrating their interconnectedness. As it turns out, she was not switching from topic to topic, she was synthesizing all these different subtopics and fitting them together to explore their impact on those "babies from Englewood" she wanted to serve and save.

Without knowing it, Kim was a master at design thinking. Design thinking is all about utilizing creative exploration to generate out-of-the-box solutions to complex problems. In *Change by Design: How Design Thinking Transforms Organizations and Inspires Innovation*, Tim Brown, CEO of IDEO, describes how the design process can be implemented by leaders in any field to tackle difficult and important problems. Brown recommends tapping into "childish pursuits" like the power of "prototyping." in order to "unlock our imaginations and open our minds to new possibilities."[37] Brown explains that "anything tangible that lets us explore an idea, evaluate it, and push it forward is a prototype. I have seen sophisticated insulin injection devices that began life as Legos. I have seen software interfaces mocked up with Post-it notes long before a line of code was written."[38] Internally referenced leaders need to provide what Brown calls "spaces of innovation"[39] or the "ideation space"[40] where employees can have time to "slow . . . down"[41] and play with ideas so that they can truly innovate. Even if employees are working from home, employers can provide permission and facilitation for innovation. This is what Kim taught me. Kim's process of exploration enabled her to be maximally creative, and her chart was a design thinking prototype, the product of exuberant play in order to address a serious complicated problem. As her professor, I learned it was my job to provide her with the time and space to do so.

Storms and Sleeplessness Are Nothing

"Storms and sleeplessness are nothing when they are over."[42] As an internally referenced leader, you cultivate an optimistic spirit.

The most important gift Catherine Morland has given me is her internally referenced optimism, joy, and magic, impenetrable by whatever is occurring in the outside world. There's no question that Catherine Morland is described as an eternal optimist. She says,

> "But we have a charming morning after it," she added, desiring to get rid of the subject; "and storms and sleeplessness are nothing when they are over. What beautiful hyacinths!—I have just learnt to love a hyacinth."[43]

Catherine really believes that the storm will always pass and there will always be a new clear sky, even if we can't quite see it. Her strength is having faith that it will eventually appear. We are told again and again that she has an affectionate, cheerful, and happy disposition. She might be the most self-sufficiently happy person in all of Jane Austen's novels. Her joy comes from the inside out and is not contingent on any external person or condition. Even after cruel General Tilney banishes her from Northanger Abbey and forces her into the public coach in the middle of the night, she weathers that storm with remarkable grace and positivity. The morning she arrives home after that storm ends, she's not bitter as many would be. Rather, she finds reasons to be appreciative and happy.

> Her father, mother, Sarah, George, and Harriet, all assembled at the door, to welcome her with affectionate eagerness, was a

sight to awaken the best feelings of Catherine's heart; and in the embrace of each, as she stepped from the carriage, she found herself soothed beyond any thing that she had believed possible. So surrounded, so caressed, she was even happy! In the joyfulness of family love everything for a short time was subdued.[44]

Harvard psychologist Daniel Gilbert has done extensive research on positivity and happiness. When asked about the most salient research on happiness, Gilbert says,

> As it turns out, people are not very good at predicting what will make them happy or how long that happiness will last. They expect positive events to make them much happier than those events actually do, and they expect negative events to make them unhappier than they actually do. In both field and lab studies, we've found that winning or losing an election, gaining or losing a romantic partner, getting or not getting a promotion, passing or failing an exam all have less impact on happiness than people think they will.[45]

Sustained happiness is often an internal state, meaning that it is not necessarily dependent on anything outside ourselves. Gilbert's work replicates the classic study by Philip Brickman, Dan Coates, and Ronnie Janoff-Bulman,[46] which asks which group of people is happier: lottery winners or amputees. It turns out that, after a year, the lottery winners and the amputees are equally happy. According to William Ury, this research suggests that "we are capable of manufacturing our own happiness" and that "the very thing we most want, happiness, is not scarce at all, but sufficient and possibly even abundant. To a great extent, it depends on us."[47]

The internally referenced leader strives to look at the world through a lens of joy, happiness, and optimism so that these states are self-generative. Whether it's loving flowers or playing with her siblings, Catherine Morland holds onto a kind of childlike magic and wonder as a way of tapping into her optimism and joy. But how can we be optimistic in the face of tragedy and even death? According to Dr. Jeannie Aschkenasy, this is when "we absolutely need to focus on the silver linings while acknowledging the painful and uncomfortable feelings."[48]

Jeannie is a clinical psychologist on staff at Rush University Children's Hospital. She calls herself "an insistent optimist no matter what"[49] and leads the wellness program for the residents and faculty of the Department of Pediatrics. Her work has been made more difficult in these times, as the emphasis on positive psychology meets the challenges of the COVID-19 pandemic.

Here's a representative scenario. It is early in April 2020, and Jeannie is presenting via Zoom to a group of pediatric residents and faculty. With a surge of COVID-19 cases in Chicago and the overcrowding at the hospital, they were being challenged to take on more risk and responsibility. Jeannie labeled this reality and provided them with a framework to understand and process their intense and varied feelings. She shared an article with them entitled "That Discomfort You're Feeling Is Grief."[50] The article is an interview with David Kessler, who along with Elisabeth Kübler-Ross, wrote *On Grief and Grieving: Finding the Meaning of Grief through the Five Stages of Loss.*[51]

Jeannie described the five stages of loss to help the residents and faculty understand that their feelings were likely the result of actual and anticipatory grief. The global pandemic had brought with it a host of losses: social connection, a feeling of safety at work and home, and routine being just a few of them. In addition, these professionals were frontline workers dealing with the uncertainty related to this new virus. Given this, Jeannie wanted to prepare these residents and faculty for the grief experience—from denial and isolation, anger, bargaining, depression, and finally to acceptance. However, she did not stop at acceptance, and instead, decided to include Kessler's recent addition of a sixth stage to the framework: finding meaning. Kessler explains, "I did not want to stop at acceptance when I experienced some personal grief. I wanted meaning in those darkest hours. And I do believe we find light in those times."[52]

Jeannie wanted to help the residents and faculty "find light and meaning even in this dark and scary time." All the tips that she had been reading focused only on those who were staying home, but she wanted to provide insight to these doctors who were working on the frontlines. She urged them to look for any and all sources of gratitude despite the grim situation they were in. She reminded them they had jobs, health insurance, access to personal protective equipment, and colleagues who cared deeply for one another. Jeannie said that "optimism is not just desired in the wake of COVID, it is absolutely necessary."[53]

The Pleasure of Walking and Breathing Fresh Air

"The pleasure of walking and breathing fresh air"[54] is essential. As an internally referenced leader, you build sacred time into your day to rest, restore, and renew.

In *The 15 Commitments of Conscious Leadership*, Jim Dethmer and his colleagues discuss the productivity impact of taking time out:

> It is difficult to convince most people that taking time off or resting during the day can actually enhance productivity. Our culture tends to think that the busier we are, the more we will produce. Research . . . [has] found that organizations whose

employees took a nap for at least thirty minutes every day were up to 35% more productive than their competitors.[55]

They go on to explain that energy is maximized when leaders honor rest and renewal. In 2007 *Harvard Business Review* published a whole article about managing energy and not time, which explains, in part, why my walk around the block helps me be more efficient and effective even under deadline.[56] According to Harvard Medical School, a multitude of relaxation practices are available to help us in our work and in our lives. These include but are not limited to breath focus, mindfulness meditation, yoga, tai chi, and guided imagery.[57] Experts also recommend taking a warm bath, listening to or playing music, writing in a journal, getting a massage, walking a dog, and even enjoying a warm decaffeinated drink.[58]

Many women who've completed my internally referenced leadership program and who agree with much of the theory and suggested practices tell me that it's easy for unmarried (and fictive) and unemployed Catherine Morland to skip through the tulips; but they wonder how in the heck they can do it without the support of their employers and the other stakeholders in their lives. I remind them that *internally referenced leadership* comes from within, not from without. It's important to me that none of the principles and suggested practices in this book be contingent on any external person or situation.

Cookie Weber was one such skeptic. A very involved mother with a busy interior design business, Cookie already "felt guilty enough" for spending "time she did not have" in a women's empowerment group. She said there was "no way in hell" she had time "just for herself" on a regular basis; she was too busy "worrying and attending to everyone else." When asked about what she did for rest and renewal, Cookie laughed out loud with a

combination snort and guffaw. She explained that when she became so "burnt out, utterly depleted, and totally drained," she
retreated to what she called her separate "apartment," which was
actually a small attic room in her house where she would nap, read
trashy books, and "totally zone out." Asked about how she felt
afterward, Cookie said she felt "guilty for taking time" for herself,
but that "it was absolutely necessary."[59]

She was dubious and disbelieving when it was suggested that
instead of retreating when she had nothing left, it might be more
effective and efficient for her to proactively incorporate some
"apartment" activities in her daily routine so she could better
meet her needs when they arose. Cookie replied that she had no
idea what her needs even were. She continued on until the next
burnout. But then Cookie found herself going through a challenging divorce. She was desperate for more energy and sanity.
She finally realized that her practice of putting everyone else first
was not going to get her through this challenging time.

Cookie ended up incorporating a couple of renewal practices
into her daily and weekly routines. No matter how much she had
to do, she reserved an hour before bed for pleasure reading. She
got a new dog, which she named Theodore Epstein Weber (after
the famous baseball savant, of course) and committed to taking
him for a walk every morning before she checked her email. Finally, she joined a women's group that met weekly. Cookie was
"pleasantly surprised" by how her investment in these seemingly
small but strictly followed activities was paying off in increased
energy, patience, and grace for "all the crap" going on in her life.
In fact, according to her, putting her own "oxygen mask on first
enabled her to do everything better" for herself, her clients, and
especially her children. Her design company is called "Inside Job,"
and now so is her life.[60]

Of course, it is easier to have regular rest and renewal during the workday when you work for yourself or you run your organization. But because regular replenishment is critical for all employees and for an institution writ large, the most effective leaders provide time and space for the people who work for them to regularly recharge and, as a result, to achieve balance in their lives.

Jennifer Hyman is a leader who has recently learned the value of replenishment for herself and her staff. She is CEO and cofounder of the billion-dollar company Rent the Runway, which she started in 2009 after watching her sister agonize over buying an expensive outfit for a wedding. She is also a well-known advocate for protection against sexual harassment and for the fair treatment of workers in the tech industry. Jennifer participates on panels and in conferences related to women in business and company culture. While her business and business model have been negatively affected by the pandemic, she points out that one of the wonderful silver linings of everyone working from home has been the discovery of the importance of family and balance, especially for women.

Jennifer readily admits what COVID has taught her: that we as a society have been too focused on business and that being home has been a great gift.

> What this period of time has proven, is that, actually, I can be a fantastic team member and leader when I'm with my family, when I'm at home, when I'm doing other things that I love. And so hopefully we'll look back on these moments and remember that there are things just way more important than work.[61]

So many working women struggle with work-life balance. For some, working from home can help in this regard; yet for others, it can make all the demands that much more difficult. But whatever and wherever the challenge, Catherine Morland energy and renewal can make all the difference.

According to the aforementioned article in *Harvard Business Review* entitled "Manage Your Energy, Not Your Time," Tony Schwartz and Catherine McCarthy of *The Energy Project* explain that many organizations now regularly attend to the physical, emotional, and spiritual energy of their employees.[62] A recent *New York Times* article extolled the benefits of "fallow time." Bonnie Tsui writes about how we are better at our jobs and our lives when we rest, refuel and renew. She makes an important distinction between "boredom" and what she calls "active refueling." Specifically, she says,

> Reading a book, visiting a museum, wandering out to people-watch at the park. . . . And I'm not talking about vacation or weekends. I'm talking about a more regular practice, built into our understanding of what work is. Fallow time is part of the work cycle, not outside of it. . . . It can feel indulgent. It can feel . . . lazy. But the difference between lazing around and laissez-faire is that I'm actually going about the business of my business.[63]

Finally, the article, which appeared in the Smarter Living section, also mentioned that in order to implement the renewal that they were advocating, the staff of Smarter Living took and was afforded regular breaks and rest time throughout the day. Even serious journalists at the Gray Lady can learn from Catherine Morland, who teaches us how to rest and renew.

How to Put More Catherine Morland in Your Life

You can put more Catherine Morland in your life by remembering that a dreaming, passionate nature and love of life can be a potent force. Catherine reminds us to use our right brain not just as refuge but also as a rich inner resource. Channeling Catherine, you tap into your inner childlike wonder and sense of play to achieve greater creativity and flow in your adult pursuits and professional life. Finally, Catherine encourages us to shore up our optimistic spirit and cheerfulness by building sacred time into our day to rest, restore, and renew—whether practicing yoga, meditating, exercising, listening to music, reading, painting, walking the dog, or doing anything in nature. Henry Thoreau wrote in *Walden*, "I frequently tramped eight or ten miles through the deepest snow to keep an appointment with a beech tree, or a yellow birch, or an old acquaintance among the pines."[64] Catherine Morland would agree than an appointment with a tree or a hyacinth can be the most important engagement of all.

Exercises for Operationalizing Principle 5

➤——→

1. Incorporate Sacred Rest into Your Routine.

Whether it is yoga or walking your dog or reading your favorite Jane Austen novel, how can you include sacred rest and regeneration time every day? And if not daily, every week? I meet my very close friends for a coffee or Zoom every Wednesday morning, and I will miss it *only* if it's an absolute emergency. I need to treat this time as sacred; it refuels me for everything else in my week.

2. Define Renewal Space at Work and at Home.

How can you create literal and figurative renewal space for yourself at home and at work and in your home office if you work from home? Do you set boundaries of when you are on and off the job? Be honest. Do you check email and Slack on evenings and weekends? Do you honor your work colleagues during those same sacred times?

3. Bring Your Inner Child to Work Day.

Close your eyes and imagine yourself at eight years old, playing your favorite game, whether swinging, pretending, playing a board game, or creating arts and crafts. See yourself completely immersed, present, and swept away in your pursuit. Can you bring that energy to your work? Can you bring that energy to your life? How can you tap into that energy every day? What are those activities that make you feel good and energize you no matter what? Now, ask yourself, what are those things that perpetually suck your energy and waste your time? Can you eliminate those draining activities little by little from your life to make more time for the enriching experiences—to make more time for that inner child?

4. Play Your Problem.

Think of a problem at work with your organization. Instead of the usual serious, worried, war-room approach, how can you use play? How can you play the problem, utilizing a right-brain activity to inspire greater creativity, flow, and out-of-the box thinking? How can cooperative play among colleagues promote a synergistic brainstorming session? How can you use crafts to build something through Constructive Play that will facilitate a creative problem-solving process? What about Storytelling Play to write a narrative that reflects a new way of thinking and creative solutions? Take pictures of your process and share your experience.

6

She Thinks "A Little Too Well of Herself"

Like Emma Woodhouse from *Emma*, constantly be
willing to learn from an internal place of openness
and humility rather than from a stance of
perfection and superiority.

Meet Emma Woodhouse

Jane Austen famously describes that Emma Woodhouse, "handsome, clever, and rich, with a comfortable home and happy disposition, seemed to unite some of the best blessings of existence; and had lived nearly twenty-one years in the world with very little to distress or vex her."[1] Austen suggests, however, that this privileged existence ultimately leads to her downfall because the "real evils indeed of Emma's situation were the power of having rather too much her own way, and a disposition to think a little too well of herself."[2]

While, admittedly, "it is very difficult for the prosperous to be humble,"[3] Emma's journey is to learn this virtue. While Miss Taylor, Emma's longtime governess and close friend, is herself an example of modesty, she, like so many in Emma's orbit, bolsters

Emma's self-importance. Miss Taylor is soon to be married to widower Mr. Weston. While Emma will miss living with her dear friend, she takes pleasure and credit for the fact that she was the one who made the match. Emma is now in search of a new daily companion, who is worthy of her but is, at the same time, subordinate in situation and personality, in order not to threaten Emma's notions of her own superiority. It also helps if it is a person whom Emma can take on as a "project" and object of her benevolent manipulation and improvement. Harriet Smith seems the ideal person to take on this role.

Harriet is Emma's tabula rasa. Her parentage is unknown, although Emma imagines that her father is a gentleman, as her education at the Goddard School has been fully provided for, albeit anonymously. When Emma learns that Harriet is about to accept the proposal of a tenant farmer named Robert Martin, she manipulates her to refuse him, claiming that Emma would not be able to socialize with someone so socially inferior. When Mr. Knightley—a long-time family friend and the brother-in-law of Emma's sister, Isabella—finds out about this, he is furious and chastises her for her scheming condescension. He asserts that Robert Martin, his tenant farmer, is a very honorable man and that Harriet's life would be greatly improved by marrying him for many reasons, including her lack of legitimate parentage.

Austen explains that Emma's relationship with Mr. Knightley is more than brother-in-law and sister-in-law. He insists on telling her "truths."[4] He is the only one who dares to criticize Emma and whom Emma, in turn, looks to for approval. While Emma is taken aback by Mr. Knightley's harsh attack, she pushes forward with her plan to improve Harriet's social status by fixing her up with Mr. Elton, the local vicar. Emma, often prone to delusion, erroneously assumes that Mr. Elton is interested in Harriet when he is actually romantically pursuing Emma. Emma is characteristically clueless ('90s film reference intended) about Mr. Elton's obvious intentions until she finds herself alone with him in a carriage on Christmas, when he declares his love, foists himself on her, and utterly demeans Harriet for good measure. Emma rejects Mr. Elton; he disappears and later returns with another rich society woman as a wife.

While Harriet is distraught at Mr. Elton's repudiation of her, Emma is happily distracted by the arrival of two intriguing and frustrating figures. Frank Churchill is the son of Mr. Weston, who has been adopted as the heir of his wealthy and controlling aunt. For months he has promised to visit his father and his father's new wife, but his aunt has always found a way to disrupt the plan. Meanwhile, Emma has created a fantasy of him in her head as the ideal suitor whose talents and prospects in life are worthy of her own.

Jane Fairfax's prospects are quite the opposite. She is described as more talented, beautiful, and hardworking than Emma but not nearly as fortunate, as Jane is the poor, orphaned niece of Miss Bates, the poor woman who is friends with everyone in genteel society and lives with her aging, sick mother. It seems that her only prospect in life is to be a governess. Instead of being gracious about Jane's plight, Emma is jealous and condescending of Jane's long-standing superior talent and empathy from the community. Frank gossips with Emma about Jane, and they end up spreading suggestive rumors about Jane having an illicit affair.

Mr. Knightley notices a strange connection between Jane and Frank, which vexes Emma. She erupts at a picnic at Box Hill, where she publicly humiliates Miss Bates. When Mr. Knightley chastises her for her terrible behavior toward the good, kind, and vulnerable Miss Bates, whose life circumstances are much worse than Emma's, Emma, almost for the first time in her life, feels real shame and true contrition. "As she reflected more, she seemed but to feel it more,"[5] and this true contrition causes her to finally access her humility and shame. She pays Miss Bates a visit the next day to apologize and learns that Jane has secured a position as a governess. Distraught, Jane refuses to see Emma or receive her gifts. Emma feels sincere regret at her ungenerous behavior and thoughts about Jane.

A reformed Emma is unselfishly happy for Jane when Frank's overbearing aunt dies and his uncle grants permission for him to marry her. Jane and Frank had been secretly engaged all this time, and his flirtation and gossip with Emma was merely a pretext to protect his inheritance. Emma is concerned that Harriet will be disappointed, since she thought Frank might be interested in her. Instead, Harriet explains that she is fond of Mr. Knightley since he's been so kind to her. Mr. Knightley, however, is interested in someone else. Jane and Frank's awareness liberates him to express his pent-up love for a very imperfect and human Emma. Thus, Emma's spiritual journey ends in terms of her realizing that she is indeed imperfect and human and has met her match in Mr. Knightley, who is someone who does not put her on a fake pedestal.

A Little Too Well of Herself

Emma Woodhouse thinks "a little too well of herself"[6] and is thus a "heroine whom no one but myself will much like,"[7] wrote Austen. In Emma, Austen created an unlikeable heroine based on arrogance and a total lack of self-awareness. As an internally referenced leader, you engage in the most important component of emotionally intelligent primal leadership: self-awareness of the areas in which you need to grow.

My son, Josh, is a philosophy major at the University of Chicago. I am a very biased mother, who believes he is one of the smartest and kindest old souls on the planet and knows a lot of stuff. He's been a philosopher since he was little and has always engaged in the meta conversation in which he talks about talking and thinks about thinking. As it turns out, according to E. M. Dadlez, "Jane Austen has always been something of a philosophical favorite."[8] Her character of Emma provides an example we can discuss and debate, including the philosophical notions of agency, autonomy, shame, and maturity. Through Josh, I discovered *Jane Austen's "Emma": Philosophical Perspectives*, edited by Dadlez. It surprised Josh that there was so much philosophy to discuss about Emma; from the very beginning of the novel Josh said she was the last person he could ever spend time with. Indeed, Austen admits that Emma "thinks a little too well of herself" and that she created a character "whom no one but [Austen herself] will much like."[9] Richard Eldridge says that "Emma's character constitutes, then, in its fitful, incomplete, but genuine development, a study in the nature and possibility of self-understanding, for creatures such as us who share her tendencies."[10] Thus, Emma causes us to confront the paradoxes of why we like the unlikeable and admire the unadmirable. From the discipline of leadership, it makes sense because Emma represents the importance of growth. She can inspire the internally referenced leader to be a lifelong learner, who comes to realize she will always be a work in progress.

One of the most important attributes for any leader is a continuous self-awareness of her weak spots as well as the areas in herself and her organization that are in need of improvement. In their book, *Primal Leadership: Unleashing the Power of Emotional Intelligence, New York Times* best-selling author Daniel Goleman and his colleagues Richard Boyatzis and Annie McKee developed the Theory of Primal Leadership, which articulates and operationalizes the critical Emotional Intelligence attributes that leaders need to be effective. One of the most important attributes is an accurate self-assessment of one's strengths and limitations as a leader and a human being. They explain,

> Accurate self-assessment. Leaders with high self-awareness typically know their limitations and strengths, and exhibit a sense of humor about themselves. They exhibit a gracefulness in learning where they need to improve, and welcome constructive criticism and feedback. Accurate self-assessment lets a leader know when to ask for help and where to focus in cultivating new leadership strengths.[11]

The most effective leaders I know say easily and often, "We got it wrong; let me learn how to make it better." Take for example Vicky Tsai, the successful founder of the $500 million skin care company Tatcha. She shares that her great success is due in part to dealing with problems, complaints, and mistakes in order to improve and innovate and keep making herself and her organization better. This began with her very first job after business school, working at Starbucks headquarters. The company implemented an immersive training program for all its corporate hires; they began their employment, no matter the position they'd been hired for, by working on the coffee line. Vicky remembers the experience as being terrifying and illuminating: "It's really, really stressful to make coffee for people when you don't know how—they get angry! . . . I spent most of my day either disappointing customers or washing dishes."[12]

This experience helped Vicky become a corporate leader who is very successful yet also refreshingly humble. Perhaps this is one of the keys to her success. She tries to instill this openness to criticism in everyone who starts working for her. She says, "To this day, I ask that everybody who works at our company starts in the warehouse. . . . The closer you are to the client, the more you understand what's working and not working. . . . I largely don't use email anymore, but I get all the ones that go to info@tatcha .com filtered into a folder that I will read—every single question, complaint, suggestion, compliment."[13] Even after her many years of success, Vicky is fully aware that she doesn't know everything. Conversely in the world of Jane Austen's *Emma*, because she believes she knows everything, Emma does not inquire, examine data, or seek out other perspectives. She surrounds herself with subordinate sycophants, who confirm her hasty, conclusory, and often wrong opinions. Shapard points out that, through the course of the novel, "Mr. Knightley will prove consistently to be more accurate than Emma . . . because he's more careful and less inclined to jump to conclusions and engage in fanciful speculations."[14]

Austen warns us about Emma's know-it-all affect and the disastrous impact it has on other people's lives as well as her own. Whether it is attempting to play matchmaker or "matchbreaker" for the illegitimate Harriet Smith, destroying perhaps her only chance of a happy marriage, or spinning scandalous lies about Jane Fairfax and damaging her reputation, Emma's lack of humility and self-awareness have the potential to ruin people's lives no matter her intentions. We worry about powerful people like Emma, who believe they know everything and will not listen to other points of view, read the research, or question their own judgment.

David Shapard has said, "The need for self-knowledge is a crucial part of the reformation of a Jane Austen heroine. . . . [Emma] has been the principal author of her trouble [and her recognition of this] represents an important step in the direction of better self-knowledge."[15] It's the journey from lack of self-awareness to self-awareness. It's the journey from knowing everything to realizing, in a state of humility, there will always be a lot to learn. This is also part of the internally referenced leader's journey; she strives to understand how she can grow, improve, and know that, as a lifelong learner, she is never done.

Bharat Tandon compares the "capricious and superficial employment" of Emma's imagination to the "rooted 'understanding'" of Knightley.[16] Emma's self-awareness develops through the course of the novel, and she achieves the rooted understanding by paradoxically acknowledging that she *doesn't* understand and there *is* more to learn. An internally referenced leader has the self-awareness to know that she doesn't always know.

To Be Humble

"It is very difficult for the prosperous to be humble."[17] As an internally referenced leader, you strive for the highest, most evolved level of leadership by blending the paradoxical combination of humility and will.

The humility Emma learns during the course of the novel is resonant with *Good to Great* author Jim Collins's conception of Level 5 Leadership. Collins's hierarchy of Level 1 Leadership to Level 5 Leadership represents an evolution of growth, effectiveness, and knowledge. Level 1 leaders are "highly capable" in using their "knowledge and skills" to contribute to their organization. Level 2 leaders are "contributing team members" who "work effective[ly] with others" to achieve "group objectives." Level 3 leaders are "competent managers" who "organize people and resources" in the "efficient pursuit of predetermined objectives." Level 4 leaders are "effective leaders" who "vigorous[ly]" commit to the "pursuit of a clear and compelling vision" and stimulate "the group to high performance standards."

On the face of it, Collins's description of Level 5 Leadership is counterintuitive. People assume it takes someone with a larger-than-life, big personality, but Level 5 Leaders are a study in duality. They are modest and willful. The Level 5 leader builds an enduring greatness through a paradoxical combination of personal humility plus professional will.[18]

Collins's discovery of Level 5 Leadership is research based and comes from a massive project asking one key question, "Can a good company become a great company, and if so, how?" To address that question, his research team examined companies that "shifted from good performance to great performance and also sustained that great performance." Their statistically significant empirical finding is fascinating. Their research showed that this transformation took a lot of things, including getting the right people and instilling a culture of discipline; but the one component that was absolutely necessary in every instance was having a Level 5 leader at the helm. Collins explains, "Good-to-great transformations don't happen without Level 5 leaders at the helm."[19]

Like Emma, the internally referenced leader does not necessarily come out of her original package with humility; but at some point along the line, she is knocked off a perch and learns it. She learns by asking questions, being reflective, thinking critically, and surrounding herself with people other than the echo chamber; she learns through honest self-assessment. Dadlez has suggested that "*Emma* is also unusual in that it presents a female character with flaws more commonly considered masculine: boldness, overconfidence, taking charge of others' lives. Hubris."[20]

Some experts posit that humility in leadership may come easier to women than men. In a *Harvard Business Review* article entitled *7 Lessons Men Can Learn from Women*, authors Cindy Gallop, founder and CEO of IfWeRanTheWorld, and Tomas Chamorro-Premuzic, Chief Talent Scientist at ManpowerGroup and professor of business psychology, urge male leaders to learn humility from female leaders. They note that "there are well-established gender differences in humility, and they favor women. . . . Without humility it will be very hard for anyone in charge to acknowledge their mistakes, learn from experience, take into account other people's perspectives, and be willing to change and get better."[21]

In her popular article in *Forbes* entitled "What Do Countries with the Best Coronavirus Responses Have in Common? Women Leaders," Avivah Wittenberg-Cox, CEO of 20-First, a global gender-balance consultancy, cites the dramatic difference in responding to the COVID-19 pandemic from countries with female leaders as opposed to male leaders. She argues that Germany, Taiwan, New Zealand, Iceland, Finland, Norway, and Denmark are "gifting us an attractive alternative way of wielding power," which allows for honest reflection on our performance and efficacy as leaders rather than the "terrifying trifecta of authoritarianism: blame-'others,' capture-the-judiciary, [and] demonize-the-journalists."[22] Wittenberg-Cox suggests that these female leaders are more interested in humbly serving and saving their constituents than protecting their own political power. By establishing trust through honest communication, they effectively protect their people and unify their countries.

These effective and reflective female leaders can be compared to former British prime minister Margaret Thatcher, who was the opposite. In an article in *Harvard Business Review* entitled "Thatcher's Greatest Strength Was Her Greatest Weakness," Robert Kaiser and Robert Kaplan state that her steadfastness, tenacity, and determination were both attributes and faults. They explain that "it was overdoing those strengths that made Thatcher so divisive. She could be obstinate, stubborn, uncompromising; what *The Economist* called a 'prim control freak.' . . . It was pointless to contradict or challenge her. She denied herself a loyal opposition—a counterforce to keep her honest, to challenge thinking, to test out ideas, and elevate understanding." While very effective in many regards, Thatcher's unwillingness to constructively examine herself and learn the truth may have undermined her ability to be even more successful.[23]

I Will Tell You Truths

"I will tell you truths while I can."[24] As an internally referenced leader, you have frank conversations with others and yourself from a place of trust and vulnerability.

According to Wittenberg-Cox, one of the chief characteristics that distinguish female leadership is the courage to be utterly transparent and truthful. For example, Germany's chancellor, Angela Merkel, took COVID-19 very seriously from the onset and told her country that it would infect more than half of its population. Wittenberg-Cox says that in this spirit of transparency, "testing began right from the get-go. Germany jumped right over the phases of denial, anger, and disingenuousness we've seen elsewhere."[25]

It takes political courage and vulnerability to communicate difficult truths in ways that inform and inspire. According to Michaela Kerrissey, assistant professor of management at Harvard School of Public Health, and Amy Edmondson, professor of leadership and management at Harvard Business School, in their article in *Harvard Business Review* entitled "What Good Leadership Looks Like during This Pandemic," effective leaders like New Zealand prime minister Jacinda Ardern have been able to communicate difficult, informative news while at the same time inspiring hope and a sense of camaraderie. The authors laud Ardern's early national address to her worried nation:

> I understand that all of this rapid change creates anxiety and uncertainty. Especially when it means changing how we live. That's

why today I am going to set out for you as clearly as possible, what you can expect as we continue to fight the virus together.[26]

Ardern illustrates what best-selling author and professor of social work and management Brené Brown would call dropping "the armor" in order to communicate with "heart and emotion, especially vulnerability" in order to create a dynamic of mutual trust.[27]

Citizens have already come to know this from Ardern. In the wake of the worst mass killing in New Zealand's history, the prime minister was praised for responding with a pragmatic idealism, which was the result of using that vulnerability to reflect on what needed changing in her government and in her country. Within days of the shooting, Ardern proposed and passed New Zealand's first meaningful gun legislation in decades, and only one member of parliament voted against it. She also had discussions with business and tech leaders formulating a strategy that utilized the involvement of tech companies to address the proliferation of gun violence in New Zealand and the world. Two months after the Christchurch shootings, her team came up with "Christchurch Call," a commitment by governments and tech companies to eliminate terrorist extremist content online. Nick Pickles, head of global public-policy strategy at Twitter, highlighted Ardern's "willingness to convene honest and sometimes difficult conversations" as a key factor in her success.[28]

An internally referenced leader's ability to engage in critical self-reflection requires that she also has the ability to conduct two-way, frank conversations in a spirit of vulnerability and trust and with an open heart—and, sometimes, a willingness to have that heart broken open. This was a key path for Emma in moving toward growth after her incident of cruelty on Box Hill, when she publicly humiliated Miss Bates, one of the kindest and most suffering members of her community.

Unsparingly curt, Mr. Knightley severely reproaches Emma, which does break her open in a way that causes much pain and much growth.

Mr. Knightley chastises Emma with utter frankness:

> "How could you be so unfeeling to Miss Bates? How could you be so insolent . . . to a woman of her character, age, and situation?—Emma, I had not thought it possible . . . .
> . . . Her situation should secure your compassion. It was badly done, indeed! . . . This is not pleasant to you, Emma—and it is very far from pleasant to me; but I must, I will,—I will tell you truths while I can, satisfied with proving myself your friend by very faithful counsel, and trusting that you will some time or other do me greater justice than you can do now."[29]

Listening to Mr. Knightley with vulnerability and her whole heart, Emma transforms in this moment from a so-called "perfect" caricature into a real human being. The transition is profound:

> She was vexed beyond what could have been expressed—almost beyond what she could conceal. Never had she felt so agitated, mortified, grieved, at any circumstance in her life. She was most forcibly struck. The truth of his representation there was no denying. She felt it at her heart. How could she have been so brutal, so cruel to Miss Bates!—How could she have exposed herself to such ill opinion in any one she valued! And how suffer him to leave her without saying one word of gratitude, of concurrence, of common kindness!
> . . . Emma felt the tears running down her cheeks almost all the way home, without being at any trouble to check them, extraordinary as they were.[30]

Stuart Tave discusses the significance of this poignant scene of her being broken open and emerging as a real human being:

The more she reflects the more she feels it. There is no laughter now as Emma feels the tears running down her cheeks and is at no trouble to check them. They are extraordinary. We have never seen them before.

The effect this time, unlike her previous ineffective resolutions, is a warmth of "true" contrition that leads to a change in her regular action.... The act of conveying the truth from eye to eye in a novel where truth has been so distorted by the eye, by the word, by the act, is a moment of great emotion. Mr. Knightley looks at her with a glow of regard, understanding that she has heard the truths he spoke, and she is warmly gratified.

The moment produces one of the most touching gestures in Jane Austen.[31]

This is Emma's *Pinocchio* moment, when she becomes a real human being. Through a truly frank exchange, Emma is awakened as if for the first time. She listens to Mr. Knightley with her head and with her heart. Kathleen Anderson describes the incident at Box Hill providing "the long-caged Emma ingresses into a kind of moral-psychological birth canal in search of maturation."[32]

Sr. Frances Ryan, PhD, a Catholic nun and emeritus faculty member at DePaul University and former director of its counseling program, believes that this kind of growth can take place throughout someone's life and can truly be beautiful. She saw this firsthand through her work at Alexian Brothers Bonaventure House. Bonaventure House is a home for people with AIDS and provides them counseling and support services. Sr. Frances brought her childhood friend, the late Cardinal George, to Bonaventure House, which was a transformative experience for them both. She said that when Cardinal George said mass for the patients at Bonaventure, "his heart opened in miraculous ways," and he had a new appreciation for the "beautiful souls" who have been suffering and marginalized for so long.[33]

Reflecting More, Feeling More

"As she reflected more, she seemed but to feel it more."[34] As an internally referenced leader, you have a growth mindset and commit to lifelong learning.

Emma is the poster child for both the Fixed Mindset and the Growth Mindset identified (and named) by Carol Dweck. Dweck utilizes a key question, among other indicators, to distinguish those with a Fixed Mindset from those with a Growth Mindset: "If you had to choose, which would it be? Loads of success and validation or lots of challenge?"[35] Emma at the beginning of the novel is squarely Fixed Mindset. The first line of the novel, in an ironic sense, is all about her success and validation and her need for success and validation. But after the incident on Box Hill, which in a very healthy way kicked her ass, she transforms into a Growth Mindset, preferring challenge.

Another question Dweck uses to distinguish Fixed Mindset from Growth Mindset asks individuals about the quality of relationships they want to have in their lives:

> People also have to decide what kinds of relationships they want: ones that bolster their egos or ones that challenge them to grow? Who is your ideal mate? We put this question to young adults, and here's what they told us.
> People with the fixed mindset said the ideal mate would:
> Put them on a pedestal.
> Make them feel perfect.
> Worship them.[36]

That is pre-Box-Hill-Emma's relationship with everyone in her orbit except for her eventual true love, Mr. Knightley. Austen's famous first line ironically enshrines Emma's fixed qualities, something everybody in that community is doing except for her true mate, Mr. Knightley. People with a Growth Mindset "hoped for a different kind of partner. They said their ideal mate was someone who would: [s]ee their faults and help them to work on them[;] [c]hallenge them to become a better person."[37] This is Emma's post–Box Hill relationship with Mr. Knightley. It is also what the internally referenced leader prefers.

Dweck explains that it is detrimental for an organization when leaders have a Fixed Mindset and are preoccupied with their own image of all-knowing perfection and power. She says it's crucial that organizations choose leaders with a Growth Mindset and that leaders choose organizations with a Growth Mindset culture:

> CEOs face this choice all the time. Should they confront their shortcomings or should they create a world where they have none? Lee Iacocca chose the latter. He surrounded himself with worshipers, exiled the critics—and quickly lost touch with where his field was going. Lee Iacocca had become a non-learner.
>
> But not everyone catches the CEO disease. Many great leaders confront their shortcomings on a regular basis. Darwin Smith, looking back on his extraordinary performance at Kimberly-Clark, declared, "I never stopped trying to be qualified for the job."[38]

Internally referenced leaders like Emma, ultimately, are committed to self-improvement—either from the start or after they have been chastened and learned through experience.

Leah was a student of mine who, while very talented and well-intentioned, needed some Emma Woodhouse chastening. She had been a star her whole life, having graduated summa cum laude from an Ivy League school and then been admitted to the prestigious Teach for America (TFA) program. TFA is a not-for-profit that recruits students from elite colleges and universities to serve as teachers in low-income communities. It provides its corps members an accelerated alternative certification program that involves an intensive summer of training before being placed in the classroom as basically a full-fledged teacher. TFA is well funded and has been praised for doing a lot of good work, as well as having a great impact with traditionally marginalized students and communities. It has provided much-needed innovation, energy, and investment in the field.

But while Teach for America has done a lot of good for the field of education and has enhanced the prominence and prestige of teaching and education, it has also faced some serious criticism and controversy. The program has been faulted for not valuing traditional teachers, traditional teaching, and the disadvantaged communities in which they live. The relationship between TFA and teachers' unions, especially, is very strained. TFA has been accused of siphoning union jobs away from teachers who have been trained and traditionally certified for years. Further, TFA alums have been seen as architects of a larger anti–public school reform agenda to expand charter schooling and to institute oppressive teacher evaluations, as well as to aggressively promote efforts to recruit teachers from nontraditional avenues.[39]

Over the years, I knew many TFA alums like Leah, who were dedicated to educational reform and truly wanted to improve kids' lives for the better. Sometimes, however, Leah had a difficult time collaborating with and even listening to her classmates, many of whom were union teachers of color. Although I tried helping her reflect on this while she was enrolled in our program, she was impenetrable and could act as if she knew more than anyone else, especially me. Other professors in the program observed a similar pattern with Leah; one even compared her to Tracy Flick from the film *Election*. My graduation gift to her was a copy of Stephen Covey's *7 Habits of Highly Effective People*, whose Habit 5—Seek First to Understand, Then to Be Understood— I was hoping she would absorb in her new job as a principal.[40]

It took a few years for her to realize she needed to listen and learn but she ultimately did. After graduating from our program, Leah was the new principal of a school that needed to be turned around. It wasn't going well. She called to ask for advice. She reached out to me because she couldn't "get the faculty on board and desperately needed help."[41] I suggested that she meet with the faculty to get to the root of the problem. It was implicit in her answer that she had little to no relationship with her faculty. I knew I needed to get into the room with them. When I met with small groups of faculty at her school, I was not surprised to learn that Leah had never talked to them about who they are, what they need, and what their visions for improving the school were. Moreover, one African American teacher I spoke with described Leah as "an upper-middle-class white woman who thinks because she worked for TFA she knows what's best for low-income black kids."[42]

When I debriefed Leah and read this quote to her, she refused to believe it at first and then became angry. We sat in silence for a while. Then she brought up Stephen Covey's Habit 5. She realized she was never going to get anywhere if she didn't learn to listen. Really listen. Leah began a serious listening tour with faculty that started to turn both her school and her outlook around. It has been several years since then, and she tells me that she is still listening and learning and feeling much more unsure than she did when she was in graduate school. She recently sent me a quote from *White Fragility* by Robin DiAngelo and indicated that this is what she is working on now:

> To interrupt white fragility, we need to build our capacity to sustain the discomfort of not knowing, the discomfort of being racially unmoored, the discomfort of racial humility. Our next task is to understand how the forces of racial socialization are

constantly at play. The inability to acknowledge these forces inevitably leads to the resistance and defensiveness of white fragility.[43]

This showed me that Leah is indeed learning from a place of humility.

Putting More (Humble) Emma in Your Life

In order to put more (humble) Emma in your life, constantly be willing to learn from an internal place of openness and humility rather than project and misbelieve fixed perfection. Admit that you could be wrong, and don't always have the answers, and be open and willing to learn from those around you. Engage in the most important component of emotionally intelligent primal leadership: self-awareness of the areas in which you need to grow. Strive to lead with humility and will. Have frank conversations with others and yourself from a place of trust and vulnerability. Live and love with a growth mindset and a commitment to life-long learning.

Exercises for Operationalizing Principle 6

1. Don't Sweat the SWOT.

Do an analysis of your strengths and opportunities for growth. Update it every year; I do it on my birthday. A SWOT analysis is comprised of honestly articulating Strengths, Weaknesses, Opportunities, and Threats. This will enable you to understand what is working for you and build on it. It will also, most importantly, allow you to understand what you need to work on in order to grow and evolve.

2. When Were You Knocked Off Your Perch?

Reflect on a time when you thought you knew everything but were knocked off your perch in dramatic fashion. What happened? Who knocked you off? How did you feel? What did you learn? Did it change how you behave or how you are an internally referenced leader?

3. Meditate on Your Tears.

Close your eyes and think about and feel into the last time you cried. Where did those tears come from? What did they mean? Have they helped you? Have they enabled you to shed what no longer serves you? Have they helped you grow?

4. Keep a Growth Journal for Work, Love, and Knowledge Every Day.

One of my very favorite things to do is write down one new thing I learned in the realms of work, love, and knowledge each day. I write this in my *Emma* Growth Journal. It could be anything from the significant to the mundane. My entry from last night: (Work) That my editing process is more effective when I read aloud; (Love) That a close friend's father is in hospice, and I've been delinquent in my contact with her; and (Knowledge) Internally referenced leadership is a constant practice of return; I'm not there all the time, but I try.

Putting It All Together

Internally Referenced Leadership as Balanced Paradox

The concept of internally referenced leadership based on the principles of Jane Austen's protagonists came to me at Old Ebbitt Grill while I was dining with my dear friend Maureen Collins in Washington, DC. We were in town to attend the Jane Austen Society of North America (JASNA) Conference in 2016. I was eating clam chowder as we were talking about the impact of Jane Austen on our personal and professional lives. I became very excited, oyster-cracker crumbs spraying from my mouth, when I realized that the most important lessons I have learned about leadership came from reading Austen.

It struck me that each one of Austen's heroines had inspired me to be a leader who felt empowered from an internal locus of control—no matter what my situation and no matter how little control I had in reality. By reading and imbibing Jane Austen all those years, I absorbed her prescriptions organically. She taught me that I could be confident, principled, playful, humble, pragmatic, and hardworking in spite of what was going on around me and how others viewed me. Through Austen, I learned that my perception of myself and my situation, which I do indeed have control over, is the most important leadership ability I could possess.

This was why reading her empowered me and made me feel strong. She taught me that strength was an inside job. Understanding how Austen's heroines operated in their own worlds enabled me to source my power from within, whether it was knowing my inherent worth and confidence in the spirit of Elizabeth Bennet; acting on my principled moral boundaries like Fanny Price; tapping into my Catherine Morland–like passion and joy; striving to be humble and willing to grow like Emma Woodhouse; working hard like Anne Elliot; or pragmatically accepting difficult realities and moving on like Elinor Dashwood. Austen's heroines are unexpectedly strong in different ways, and they inspire me to view leadership as more of a way at looking at yourself than as an external title or role.

Each heroine embodies a characteristic that not only sets her apart within the context of her novel but creates a template that has timeless resonance. Through these fictional women, I recognized the concept of internally referenced leadership and its six core principles. Being an expert in leadership and a Janeite, I realized that this Austen-inspired theory of internally referenced leadership provides a framework for helping a leader feel and act from a place of power—even when her community considers her powerless or tries to take away her power. The most influential leaders exhibit the six principles. Through these attributes, they are able to tap into an inner strength that enables them to rise above any circumstance however intractable they may seem. The six principles also have enabled me to be my unique self in whatever discordant surroundings I find myself and however disconnected I might initially feel. As Ralph Waldo Emerson said, "It is easy in the world to live after the world's opinion; it is easy in solitude to live after our own; but the great man is he who in the midst of the crowd keeps with perfect sweetness the independence of solitude."[1] Jane Austen's principles help me discover that perfect sweetness.

Then I made another discovery. The very best leaders have these (sometimes seemingly contradictory) qualities in combination. I saw that the individual characteristics connected in organic and powerful ways. The internally referenced leader is one who can strike a balance between paradoxes.

Internally Referenced Leadership

Internally Referenced Knowing for the NOW		Internally Referenced Growing for the NEXT
Anchored in SELF for Personal Present		Anchored in SELF for Collective Future

Elizabeth Bennet = Confidence ↓ (principled + playful)	&	Humility = Emma Woodhouse ↓ (acceptance + work)
Fanny Price = Principled Morals	&	Pragmatic Acceptance = Elinor Dashwood
Catherine Morland = Play Hard	&	Work Hard = Anne Elliot

How Internally Referenced
Leadership Is a Fine Balance

In looking at the chart, it is interesting to note that the attributes line up as direct paradoxes that balance each other out. Elizabeth Bennet's confidence can be balanced by Emma Woodhouse's learned humility. In fact, as discussed in chapter 6, Jim Collins's most effective leader is one who acts from a can-do will balanced by a sincere humility. Similarly, Fanny Price's principled morals and willingness to stop the action in order to do what is right can be balanced by Elinor Dashwood's pragmatic acceptance of difficult realities and her ability to problem-solve and move forward. Life, after all, is often about knowing when to stop and when to go. Anne Elliot reminds us to work hard, which should be balanced with Catherine Morland's propensity to play hard. There are many times we find ourselves working too hard, playing too hard, or worst of all, doing neither. The spirit of Anne and Catherine work together so that we can balance body and soul.

The chart reveals some other interesting patterns among the heroines and their attributes. Elizabeth Bennet is often described as principled and playful. Coincidentally, Fanny is principled, and Catherine is playful. Similarly, Emma's growth trajectory involves accepting the world and herself as they really are and working hard to become a better person. Pragmatic acceptance is very Elinor, and working hard characterizes Anne. In other words, Elizabeth can be seen as a balance between Fanny and Catherine and Emma needs to grow into a combination of Elinor and Anne.

Moreover, the attributes on the left side of the chart—Elizabeth's confidence, Fanny's principled morals, and Catherine's play—comprise what I call *Internally Referenced Knowing for the Now*. They all involve anchoring in oneself for the personal present. Elizabeth can inspire us to anchor ourselves in our inherent worthiness so that we can be confident heading into any situation. Fanny can remind us to anchor ourselves in our own moral code before we confront any external conflict. And Catherine reminds us to anchor ourselves in a spirit of childlike play, joy, and passion in the present moment in order to feel refreshed, refueled, and creative.

The attributes on the right side of the chart—Emma's learned humility, Elinor's pragmatic acceptance, and Anne's hard work—together make up the category I call *Internally Referenced Growing for the Next*. These attributes all involve anchoring in oneself for a collective future. For example, Emma reminds us to anchor in humility so that we can grow and learn from the people we interact with in order to be of real use to them at some point down the line. Elinor inspires us to accept difficult realities and keep going, as we solve the problems and ultimately get our families or our organizations to a better place. Finally, Anne can encourage hard work and delayed gratification, empowering us to enjoy our goals and upcoming rewards.

Balanced Paradox in Practice

The Internally Referenced Leadership Balanced Paradox can also be useful in forming effective and multifaceted teams. Lori

Lovens, of Innovation Savvy, specializes in cross-functional team development and training for companies all across the country. According to Lori, the best teams have that "yin-yang balance" and are always comprised of "leapers and net builders." She explains that a team would want the bias-to-action, Elinor-type colleague, who is prone to move things along, to be counterbalanced by a cautious, Fanny-type colleague, who ensures that ethics and mission are followed. Carol Henriques, principal and client partner at the global consulting company TiER1 Performance Solutions, believes that organizations as well as teams need to embody paradox and be balanced in their design and approach.

That counterbalance can also exist across companies and even across cultures. For example, I met Cassie several years ago when she was a student at Beijing Foreign Studies University, the preeminent Chinese university specializing in foreign studies. To supplement her income at that time, she worked as my translator while I did professional development with fifty-one school principals in China.

Cassie helped me navigate interesting cultural differences. When participants complimented my sessions, I would say thank you, and they always started laughing. I asked Cassie about this, and she explained that culturally Chinese were raised to be humble and always deflect compliments. Those principals and Cassie herself so embodied Emma Woodhouse's learned humility.

After one of our long workdays, Cassie took me to a bookstore to buy a Chinese translation of *Pride and Prejudice*. I ended up buying her a copy too. Cassie has since graduated and is working at a large global insurance company. She recently mentioned that she was in an awkward situation with a colleague who chastised her for offering her opinion when asked and she really had to channel Elizabeth Bennet's confidence. She thanked me for teaching her about that, and I thanked her for teaching me Emma Woodhouse's humility.

Still Working on My Ship

As I continue to work on learning humility myself, I have to acknowledge that the principles of internally referenced leadership are never mastered or perfected. Nor should they be. All human beings are works in progress, and a commitment to learning and self-improvement is ongoing. But the six principles I've gleaned from Austen's heroines have provided me an aspiration, a practice, and a lifelong curriculum.

Jane Austen still finds me in surprising places. While attending a chakra balancing for a stiff back, I was having difficulty identifying my root chakra. When the practitioner talked about how it represented our "grounding, ability to withstand challenge, and find safety," I instantly thought of Elinor Dashwood and knew what the practitioner meant. I then realized that my blocked sacral chakra reminded me of a blocked Emma, needing help relating to our emotions. In my solar plexus, I felt the confidence and power of Elizabeth Bennet. I knew the empathy and compassion in my heart chakra were worthy of Anne Elliot, but I wondered whether my throat chakra could be as clear as Fanny Price in speaking truth and setting boundaries. Finally, I was grateful that my third eye was the chakra of intuition, imagination, and the joyful Catherine Morland.

Indeed, these heroines balance me in so many ways. I reread the Austen novels every year to remind myself that, no matter what is going on in the external world or how I am being squeezed professionally or personally, I can always choose to be well in a state of internal equanimity. Austen acknowledged that life can be challenging and rough, writing, "We none of us expect to be in smooth water all our days." But she also suggests to me that if we anchor in our internally referenced self, we have the makings of a kickass boat.

Notes

Introduction.
What Would Jane Do?

1. Rebecca Morin, Sarah Elbeshbishi, and Caren Bohan, "We Can All Relate to This: Why AOC's Speech on Sexism Struck a Chord beyond Washington," *USA Today*, July 25, 2020, https://www.usatoday.com /story/news/politics/2020/07/25/aoc-speech-rebuking-ted-yoho-struck -chord-well-beyond-washington/5506707002/.
2. Andrea Kayne Kaufman, "You're Fired! Donald Trump, No Child Left Behind, and the Limits of Dissonant Leadership in Education," *Journal of Women in Educational Leadership* 3, no. 3 (July 2005): 193–212.
3. Kathleen Anderson, *Jane Austen's Women: An Introduction* (Albany: State University of New York Press, 2018), 65.
4. Anderson, 66.
5. Anderson, 82.
6. Holly Luetkenhaus and Zoe Weinstein, *Austentatious: The Evolving World of Jane Austen Fans* (Iowa City: University of Iowa Press, 2019), 45.
7. Tina Brown, "What Happens When Women Stop Leading Like Men: Jacinda Ardern, Nancy Pelosi and the Power of Female Grace," *New York Times,* March 30, 2019, https://www.nytimes.com/2019/03/30 /opinion/women-leadership-jacinda-ardern.html.
8. Jane Austen, *Persuasion*, ed. Janet Todd and Antje Blank (Cambridge: Cambridge University Press, 2013), 75.

Chapter 1.
"Universal Truths" Are Anything But

1. Jane Austen, *Pride and Prejudice,* ed. Pat Rogers (Cambridge: Cambridge University Press, 2013), 3.
2. Austen, 122.

3. Austen, 215.

4. Austen, 396.

5. Celia J. Wall and Pat Gannon-Leary, "A Sentence Made by Men: Muted Group Theory Revisited," *European Journal of Women's Studies* 6, no. 1 (1999): 21–29, https://journals.sagepub.com/doi/abs/10.1177/13505068 9900600103.

6. Austen, *Pride and Prejudice,* ed. Rogers, 3.

7. Austen, 462n1.

8. Peter Conrad, introduction to *Pride and Prejudice,* by Jane Austen (New York: Everyman's Library, 1991) xii, x.

9. Mary C. Gentile, *Giving Voice to Values: How to Speak Your Mind When You Know What's Right* (New Haven: Yale University Press, 2010), 86.

10. Bill George et al., "Discovering Your Authentic Leadership," *Harvard Business Review,* February 2007, https://hbr.org/2007/02/discovering -your-authentic-leadership.

11. Daniel Goleman, Richard Boyatzis, and Annie McKee, *Primal Leadership: Unleashing the Power of Emotional Intelligence* (Boston: Harvard Business Review Press, 2013), 253.

12. Alicia Menendez, *The Likeability Trap: How to Break Free* (New York: Harper Business, 2019), 396–97.

13. Gentile, 86–87.

14. Deborah Tannen, "The Power of Talk: Who Gets Heard and Why," *Harvard Business Review,* September-October 1995, https://hbr.org /1995/09/the-power-of-talk-who-gets-heard-and-why.

15. Austen, *Pride and Prejudice,* ed. Rogers, 121.

16. Jane Austen, *The Annotated Pride and Prejudice,* ed. David M. Shapard (New York: Anchor Books, 2012), 213nn35–36.

17. Austen, *Pride and Prejudice,* ed. Rogers, 121.

18. Austen, 121.

19. Jane Austen, *Pride and Prejudice: An Annotated Edition,* ed. Patricia Meyer Spacks (Cambridge: Belknap Press of Harvard University Press, 2010), 149n27.

20. Ivor Morris, *Mr. Collins Considered: Approaches to Jane Austen* (New York: Routledge and Kegan, 1987), 160.

21. Anderson, 112.

22. Mika Brzezinski, *Know Your Value: Women, Money, and Getting What You're Worth,* rev. ed. (New York: Hachette Books, 2018), 48.

23. Carol Gilligan, *In a Different Voice: Psychological Theory and Women's*

Development (Cambridge: Harvard University Press, 1982, 1993), xix–xx.

24. Jeanine L. Prime, Nancy M. Carter and Theresa M. Welbourne, "Women 'Take Care,' Men 'Take Charge': Managers' Stereotypic Perceptions of Women and Men Leaders," *Psychologist-Manager Journal* 12 (2009): 25–49. doi:10.1080/10887150802371799.

25. Prime, Carter, and Welbourne, 32, table 1.

26. Bethany Garner, "Female Leadership during COVID-19: What Can We Learn?" *BusinessBecause*, June 19, 2020, https://www.businessbecause.com/news/insights/7028/learn-female-leadership-covid-19.

27. Henri Nouwen (@HenriNouwen), Twitter, accessed October 26, 2017, https://twitter.com/HenriNouwen/status/923520684378198016?s=20.

28. Austen, *Pride and Prejudice,* ed. Rogers, 26, 12.

29. Austen, 430.

30. June Brought, in discussion with the author, August 26, 2018.

31. Austen, 215.

32. Austen, *The Annotated Pride and Prejudice,* ed. Shapard, 373.

33. Austen, *Pride and Prejudice,* ed. Rogers, 215.

34. Austen, *Pride and Prejudice: An Annotated Edition*, ed. Spacks, 233n25.

35. Anderson, 54.

36. Stuart M. Tave, *Some Words of Jane Austen* (Chicago: University of Chicago Press, 2019), 136.

37. Roger Fisher, William Ury, and Bruce Patton, *Getting to Yes: Negotiating Agreement without Giving In* (London: Penguin Group, 1991).

38. William Ury, *Getting to Yes with Yourself: (And Other Worthy Opponents)* (New York: HarperCollins, 2015), 3.

39. Ury, 55.

40. Austen, *Pride and Prejudice,* ed. Rogers, 215.

41. Stephen Pollan and Mark Levine, *Fire Your Boss* (New York: HarperCollins, 2004), 8.

42. Abby, in discussion with the author, November 1, 2018.

43. Kathleen Reardon, "The Memo Every Woman Keeps in Her Desk," in *HBR's 10 Must Reads on Women and Leadership* (Boston: Harvard Business Review Press, 2019), 91–92.

44. David G. Smith, Judith E. Rosenstein, and Margaret C. Nikolov, "The Different Words We Use to Describe Male and Female Leaders," *Harvard Business Review* (May 25, 2018): 2–4, https://hbr.org/2018/05/the-different-words-we-use-to-describe-male-and-female-leaders.

45. Jim Dethmer, Diana Chapman, and Kaley Warner Klemp, *The 15*

Commitment of Conscious Leadership: A New Paradigm for Sustainable Success (N.p.: Conscious Leadership Group, 2015), 237.

46. Dethmer, Chapman, and Klemp, 245.

47. Austen, *Pride and Prejudice,* ed. Rogers, 394.

48. Austen, 394–97.

49. Anderson, 192.

50. Devoney Looser, *The Making of Jane Austen* (Baltimore: John Hopkins University Press, 2017), 96–97.

51. Deepak Chopra, *The Seven Spiritual Laws of Success* (San Rafael: Amber-Allen Publishing, 1995), 26–27.

52. Austen, *Pride and Prejudice,* ed. Rogers, 396.

53. Stephen Mitchell, *Tao Te Ching* (New York: Harper Books, 1999), 53.

Chapter 1: Exercises

1. Jane Austen, *Pride and Prejudice* (New York: Harper Perennial, 2018), 186.

Chapter 2.
Being "Mistress of Myself" Ain't Easy, Sister

1. Jane Austen, *Sense and Sensibility*, ed. Edward Copeland (Cambridge: Cambridge University Press, 2013), 7.

2. Austen, 7.

3. Austen, 66.

4. Austen, 7

5. Austen, 297.

6. Austen, 150.

7. Austen, 406.

8. Ellen, in discussion with the author, December 4, 2014.

9. Austen, 7.

10. Austen, 8.

11. Jane Austen, *Sense and Sensibility*, ed. Patricia Meyer Spacks (Cambridge: Belknap, 2013), 256.

12. Jane Austen, *The Annotated Sense and Sensibility*, ed. David M. Shapard (New York: Anchor Books, 2011), 565n18.

13. Tave, 105.

14. Austen, *The Annotated Sense and Sensibility*, ed. Shapard, 255n2.

15. Diane L. Coutu, "How Resilience Works," *Harvard Business Review*, May 2002, reprinted in *HBR's 10 Must Reads Collection* (Boston: Harvard Business Review Press, 2014).

16. Austen, *Sense and Sensibility*, ed. Copeland, 7.

17. Coutu.

18. Austen, *Sense and Sensibility*, ed. Copeland, 8.

19. Austen, 7.

20. Austen, *The Annotated Sense and Sensibility*, ed. Shapard, 255.

21. Alison Beard, "Mindfulness in the Age of Complexity: An Interview with Ellen Langer," chap. 1 in *Mindfulness*, HBR Emotional Intelligence Series (Boston: Harvard Business School Publishing, 2017), 4.

22. Austen, *Sense and Sensibility*, ed. Copeland, 51.

23. Austen, 59.

24. Stephen R. Covey, *The Seven Habits of Highly Effective People* (Coral Gables: Mango Publishing, 2016), 100.

25. Covey, 101.

26. Heidi, in discussion with the author, February 8, 2019.

27. Ronald A. Heifetz and Marty Linsky, "A Survival Guide for Leaders," in *HBR's 10 Must Reads Collection* (Boston: Harvard Business Review Press, 2014), 102.

28. Heifetz and Linsky, 103.

29. Heifetz and Linsky, 102–3.

30. Heifetz and Linsky, 104.

31. Austen, *The Annotated Sense and Sensibility*, ed. Shapard, 93n11.

32. Austen, 255n7.

33. Austen, 39n15.

34. Austen.

35. Austen, *Sense and Sensibility*, ed. Spacks, 57n2.

36. Renee, in discussion with the author, May 30, 2018.

37. Sophie, in discussion with the author, April 19, 2017.

38. Austen, *Sense and Sensibility*, ed. Copeland, 24.

39. Austen, 7.

40. Austen, 154.

41. Austen, *Sense and Sensibility*, ed. Spacks, 179n13.

42. Austen, 185n10.

43. Tony, in discussion with the author, October 8, 2017.

44. Jennifer, in discussion with the author, April 10, 2019.

45. Ury, *Getting to Yes with Yourself*, 21.

46. Ury, 27.

47. Jennifer, in discussion with the author, April 10, 2019.

48. Thich Nhat Hanh, *How to Fight* (Berkeley: Parallax Press, 2017), 44.

49. Austen, *Sense and Sensibility*, ed. Spacks, 185n11.

50. Austen, *Sense and Sensibility*, ed. Copeland, 406.

51. Austen, 408.

52. Tave, 107.

53. Emily Auerbach, *Searching for Jane Austen* (Madison: University of Wisconsin Press, 2004), 109.

54. Auerbach.

55. Austen, *Sense and Sensibility*, ed. Spacks, 304.

56. Joshua D. Margolis and Paul G. Stoltz, "How to Bounce Back from Adversity," in *HBR's 10 Must Reads: On Mental Toughness* (Boston: Harvard Business Review Press, 2018), 79.

57. Margolis and Stoltz, 85.

58. Viktor Frankl, *Man's Search for Meaning* (Boston: Beacon Press, 2006).

59. Frankl, 67.

60. Frankl, 130.

61. Kathy Bresler, in discussion with the author, May 18, 2018.

62. Bresler.

63. Bresler.

64. Kathleen Medina, in discussion with the author, June 28, 2018.

Chapter 3.
In Defense of Sea-Faring Folks with Weathered Skin

1. Austen, *Persuasion*, ed. Todd and Blank, 4.

2. Austen, 22.

3. Austen, 123.

4. Austen, 28.

5. Austen, 9–10.

6. Austen, 28.

7. Austen, 269.

8. Greta Thunberg, "You're Acting Like Spoiled Irresponsible Children," European Economic and Social Committee, February 21, 2019, https://www.eesc.europa.eu/en/news-media/videos/youre-acting-spoiled-irresponsible-children-speech-greta-thunberg-climate-activist.

9. Austen, *Persuasion*, ed. Todd and Blank, 4.

10. Austen, 21–22.

11. Jane Austen, *Persuasion: An Annotated Edition*, ed. Robert Morrison (Cambridge: Belknap Press of Harvard University Press, 2011), 33n4.

12. Jane Austen, *The Annotated Persuasion*, edited by David M. Shapard (New York: Anchor Books, 2010), 3n3.

13. Austen, 37n21.

14. Austen, *Persuasion*, ed. Morrison, 4.

15. Austen, *Persuasion*, ed. Todd and Blank, 21.

16. Austen, 28.

17. Austen, 29.

18. Austen, *Persuasion*, ed. Morrison, 11.

19. Austen, *Persuasion*, ed. Todd and Blank, 6.

20. Austen, 171.

21. Jean M. Twenge and W. Keith Campbell, *The Narcissism Epidemic: Living in the Age of Entitlement* (New York: Atria Books, 2009), 7, Apple Books.

22. Aaron James, *Assholes: A Theory of Donald Trump* (New York: Penguin Random House LLC, 2016), 11, Apple Books.

23. James, 4.

24. James.

25. Michelle King, "Leaders, Stop Denying the Gender Inequity in Your Organization," *Harvard Business Review*, June 18, 2020, 4.

26. Alice H. Eagly and Linda Lorene Carli, *Through the Labyrinth: The Truth about How Women Become Leaders* (Boston: Harvard Business Review Press, 2007), 154.

27. Eagly and Carli, 155.

28. Polly Young-Eisendrath, *The Self-Esteem Trap: Raising Confident and Compassionate Kids in an Age of Self-Importance* (New York: Little, Brown, 2008), 15, Apple Books.

29. Julian Jonker and Shaun Harper, "The College Cheating Scandal: The Biggest Victim Is Public Confidence," *Knowledge @ Wharton*, March 15, 2019, https://knowledge.wharton.upenn.edu/article/college-admissions -scandal/#comments.

30. Jacque Nelson, in discussion with the author, June 1, 2018.

31. Young-Eisendrath, 46.

32. Robert K. Greenleaf, "What Is Servant Leadership?," Center for Servant Leadership, https://www.greenleaf.org/what-is-servant -leadership/.

33. Stephen Mitchell, *Tao Te Ching, A New English Version* (New York: HarperCollins e-books, 1994), 60.

34. Austen, *The Annotated Persuasion*, ed. Shapard, 317n28.

35. Austen, 100.

36. Austen, 101n4.

37. Austen, ed. Todd and Blank, 123.

38. Auerbach, 236.

39. Auerbach, 238.

40. Austen, *Persuasion*, ed. Todd and Blank, 270.

41. Austen, 261.

42. Austen, 270.

43. Daniel Goleman, "The Focused Leader," in *Focus: HBR Emotional Intelligence Series* (Boston: Harvard Business Review Press, 2018), 11.

44. Goleman, 15.

45. *Persuasion*, ed. Todd and Blank, 75.

46. Austen, 268–69.

47. Tave, 272.

48. Guy Raz, "Cisco Systems & Urban Decay: Sandy Lerner," *How I Built This with Guy Raz*, NPR, October 1, 2018, 54:11, https://www.npr.org /2018/09/28/652663380/cisco-systems-urban-decay-sandy-lerner.

49. Simon Sinek, *Leaders Eat Last: Why Some Teams Pull Together and Others Don't* (New York: Penguin Random House, 2014), 111, Apple Books.

50. Jeanine Marie Russaw, "8 Ruth Bader Ginsburg Quotes That Define the Supreme Court Justice's Legacy," *Newsweek*, September 18, 2020, https://www.newsweek.com/8-ruth-bader-ginsburg-quotes-that -define-supreme-court-justices-legacy-1471585.

51. Kevin Hogan, "Five Ways Ruth Bader Ginsburg Made a Difference, Stayed Connected to Cornell," *Ithaca Journal*, September 21, 2020, https://www.ithacajournal.com/story/news/local/2020/09/19/rbg -supreme-court-ruth-bader-ginsburg-graduate-cornell-1954-five-ways -made-difference/5841271002/.

52. United States v. Virginia, 518 U.S. 515 (1996), https://www.law.cornell .edu/supct/html/94-1941.ZO.html.

Chapter 4.
A Better Guide in Ourselves

1. Jane Austen, *Mansfield Park*, ed. John Wiltshire (Cambridge: Cambridge University Press, 2013),12.

2. Austen, 231.

3. Austen, 406.
4. Austen, 478.
5. Austen, 402.
6. Austen, 450.
7. Austen, 533.
8. Austen, 478.
9. Sharon Chuter, "How I Built Resilience: Live with Sharon Chuter," *How I Built This with Guy Raz*, July 9, 2020, 5:07, https://www.npr.org /2020/07/08/889030664/how-i-built-resilience-live-with-sharon -chuter.
10. Chuter.
11. https://uomabeauty.com/pages/about-uoma.
12. Gabby Shacknai, "Uoma Beauty's Sharon Chuter Is Holding Brands Accountable with 'Pull Up or Shut Up,'" June 8, 2020, https://www .forbes.com/sites/gabbyshacknai/2020/06/08/uoma-beautys-sharon -chuter-is-holding-brands-accountable-with-pull-up-or-shut-up/#38b33 b9370de.
13. Nicholas Epley and Amit Kumar, "How to Design an Ethical Organization: A Behavioral Approach," *Harvard Business Review*, May-June 2019, https://hbr.org/2019/05/how-to-design-an-ethical-organization.
14. Epley and Kumar.
15. Lionel Trilling, *The Moral Obligation to Be Intelligent: Selected Essays*, ed. Leon Wieseltier (New York: Farrar, Straus, and Giroux E-book, 2000), 294–95.
16. Jane Austen, *The Annotated Mansfield Park*, ed. David M. Shapard (New York: Anchor Books, 2017), 346, 481n12.
17. Tave, 194–95.
18. Steve Denning, "The Best of Peter Drucker," *Forbes*, June 2014, https:// www.forbes.com/sites/stevedenning/2014/07/29/the-best-of-peter -drucker/#3f1ad2e95a96.
19. Peter Drucker, "Managing Oneself," in *HBR's 10 Must Reads on Managing Yourself* (Boston: Harvard Business Review Press, 2010), 22.
20. Heather, in discussion with the author, March 8, 2018.
21. Austen, *Mansfield Park*, ed. Wiltshire, 109.
22. Robert Allen Iger, *The Ride of a Lifetime: Lessons Learned from 15 Years as CEO of the Walt Disney Company* (New York: Random House, 2019), Apple Books, 309.
23. Iger, 321.
24. Iger, 323.

25. Iger, 324.

26. Austen, *The Annotated Mansfield Park*, ed. Shapard, 793n20.

27. Austen, *Mansfield Park*, ed. Wiltshire, 109.

28. Austen, 274.

29. Austen, 406.

30. "Christine Blasey Ford's Opening Statement for Senate Hearing," NPR, September 26, 2018, https://www.npr.org/2018/09/26/651941113 /read-christine-blasey-fords-opening-statement-for-senate-hearing.

31. "Christine Blasey Ford's Opening Statement."

32. Howard Gardner, quoted in Bronwyn Fryer, "The Ethical Mind," *Harvard Business Review*, March 2007, https://hbr.org/2007/03/the -ethical-mind.

33. Gardner.

34. Rachel M. Brownstein, *Why Jane Austen?* (New York: Columbia University Press, 2011), 200.

35. Austen, *The Annotated Mansfield Park*, ed. Shapard, 573n32.

36. Tave, 183.

37. Austen, *Mansfield Park*, ed. Wiltshire, 231.

38. Helena Kelly, *Jane Austen, the Secret Radical* (New York: Vintage Books, 2016), 168–69.

39. Rachel Cohen, *Austen Years: A Memoir in Five Novels* (New York: Farrar, Straus and Giroux, 2020), 169–70.

40. Tave, 174.

41. Austen, *Mansfield Park*, ed. Wiltshire, 533.

42. Austen, *The Annotated Mansfield Park*, ed. Shapard, 829n2.

Chapter 4: Exercises

1. Drucker, 24–26.

Chapter 5.
"Learning to Love Is the Thing"

1. Jane Austen, *Northanger Abbey*, ed. Barbara M. Benedict and Deirdre Le Faye (Cambridge: Cambridge University Press, 2013), 178.

2. Austen, 179.

3. Austen, 178.

4. Austen.

5. Austen, 179.

6. Anderson, 186.

7. Anderson, xxiii.

8. Anderson, 214.

9. Anderson, 186.

10. Austen, *Northanger Abbey*, ed. Benedict and Le Faye, 178–79.

11. Austen, 36.

12. Tave, *Some Words of Jane Austen*, 38.

13. Auerbach, 85.

14. Auerbach.

15. Mihaly Csikszentmihalyi, *Flow* (New York: HarperCollins e-books, 1990), Apple Books, 71.

16. Csikszentmihalyi.

17. Csikszentmihalyi, 103.

18. Brigid Schulte, *Overwhelmed: Work, Love, and Play When No One Has the Time* (New York: Farrar, Straus and Giroux e-books, 2014), Apple Books, 48.

19. Schulte, 58. The second quotation is from Schulte, paraphrasing Erik Erikson.

20. Benjamin Zander and Rosamund Stone Zander, *The Art of Possibility* (New York: Penguin Books, 2002), Apple Books, 288.

21. Zander and Zander, 49.

22. Scot Osterweil, "The 4 Freedoms of Play & Learning," Playful Learning, April 25, 2007. http://playfullearning.com/4freedoms/.

23. Osterweil.

24. Dr. Donna Kiel, in discussion with the author, May 7, 2018.

25. Kiel.

26. Brendan Boyle, "6 Ways to Integrate Play into the Workplace," *Inc.*, July 2015, https://www.inc.com/brendan-boyle/play-has-a-pr-problem.html.

27. Original spelling is *extasy*.

28. Austen, *Northanger Abbey*, ed. Benedict and Le Faye, 142.

29. Tave, 38–39.

30. Kelly, 64.

31. Dethmer, Chapman, and Klemp, 205.

32. Dethmer, Chapman, and Klemp, 206.

33. Alex Liu, "Making Joy a Priority at Work," *Harvard Business Review*, July 17, 2019, 2.

34. Austen, *Northanger Abbey*, ed. Benedict and Le Faye, 178.

35. Kim Lloyd, in discussion with the author, August 17, 2018.

36. Lloyd.

37. Tim Brown, *Change by Design: How Design Thinking Transforms Organizations and Inspires Innovation* (New York: HarperCollins, 2009), 87.

38. Brown, 92.

39. Brown, 105.

40. Brown, 106.

41. Brown, 105.

42. Austen, *Northanger Abbey*, ed. Benedict and Le Faye, 178.

43. Austen.

44. Austen, 241–42.

45. Gardiner Morse, "The Science behind the Smile: An Interview with Daniel Gilbert by Gardiner Morse," in *Emotional Intelligence: Happiness* (Boston: Harvard Business Review Press, 2017), 32 –33.

46. Philip Brickman, Dan Coates, and Ronnie Janoff-Bulman, "Lottery Winners and Accident Victims: Is Happiness Relative?," *Journal of Personality and Social Psychology* 36, no. 8 (1978): 917–27, https://doi .org/10.1037/0022-3514.36.8.917.

47. Ury, 80.

48. Dr. Jeannie Aschkenasy, in discussion with the author, April 2, 2020.

49. Aschkenasy.

50. Scott Berinato, "That Discomfort You're Feeling Is Grief," *Harvard Business Review*, March 23, 2020, https://hbr.org/2020/03/that -discomfort-youre-feeling-is-grief.

51. Elisabeth Kübler-Ross and David Kessler, *On Grief and Grieving: Finding the Meaning of Grief through the Five Stages of Loss* (New York: Simon and Schuster, 2005).

52. Berinato.

53. Aschkenasy, in discussion with the author, April 2, 2020.

54. Austen, *Northanger Abbey*, ed. Benedict and Le Faye, 178.

55. Dethmer, Chapman, and Klemp, 212.

56. Tony Schwartz and Catherine McCarthy, "Manage Your Energy, Not Your Time," *Harvard Business Review*, October 2007, 22.

57. Julie Corliss, "Six Relaxation Techniques to Reduce Stress," *Harvard Health Publishing*, September 2016, updated September 10, 2019, https://www.health.harvard.edu/mind-and-mood/six-relaxation -techniques-to-reduce-stress.

58. "Stress Management: Relaxing Your Mind and Body," Michigan Medi-

cine, last modified June 28, 2018, https://www.uofmhealth.org/health
-library/uz2209.

59. Cookie Weber, in discussion with the author, July 18, 2018.

60. Weber.

61. Jennifer Hyman, in discussion with the author, May 23, 2020.

62. Schwartz and McCarthy, 65.

63. Bonnie Tsui, "You Are Doing Something Important When You Aren't
Doing Anything," *New York Times*, June 21, 2019, https://www.nytimes
.com/2019/06/21/opinion/summer-lying-fallow.html.

64. Henry David Thoreau, *Walden, Or, Life in the Woods* (United
Kingdom: Delphi Classics, 2013), IBook edition, 698–99.

Chapter 6.
She Thinks "A Little Too Well of Herself"

1. Jane Austen, *Emma*, ed. Richard Cronin and Dorothy McMillan
(Cambridge: Cambridge University Press, 2013), 3.

2. Austen.

3. Austen, 476.

4. Austen, 408.

5. Austen, 409.

6. Austen, 3.

7. Auerbach, 202.

8. E. M. Dadlez, *Jane Austen's "Emma": Philosophical Perspectives* (New
York: Oxford University Press, 2018), 1.

9. Auerbach, 202.

10. Richard Eldridge, "'A Danger at Present Unperceived': Self-
Understanding, Imagination, Emotion, and Social Stance in *Emma*,"
in *Jane Austen's "Emma": Philosophical Perspectives,* ed. E. M. Dadlez
(Oxford: Oxford University Press, 2018), 110.

11. Goleman, Boyatzis, and McKee, 253–54.

12. Jennifer Liu, "This Harvard MBA Grad Worked at a Starbucks after
Graduation—Then She Founded a Company Worth Millions," CNBC,
last modified January 13, 2020, https://www.cnbc.com/2020/01/10
/tatchas-vicky-tsai-worked-at-starbucks-after-harvard-business-school
.html.

13. Liu.

14. Jane Austen, *The Annotated Emma*, edited by David M. Shapard (New
York: Anchor Books, 2012), 65n18.

15. Austen, 733.

16. Jane Austen, *Emma: An Annotated Edition*, ed. Bharat Tandon (Cambridge: Belknap Press of Harvard University Press, 2012), 68.

17. Austen, *Emma*, ed. Cronin and McMillan, 476.

18. Jim Collins, "Level 5 Leadership: The Triumph of Humility and Fierce Resolve," *Harvard Business Review*, January 2001, https://hbr.org/2001/01/level-5-leadership-the-triumph-of-humility-and-fierce-resolve-2.

19. Collins.

20. Dadlez, 20.

21. Tomas Chamorro-Premuzic and Cindy Gallop, "7 Leadership Lessons Men Can Learn from Women," *Harvard Business Review*, April 1, 2020, https://hbr.org/2020/04/7-leadership-lessons-men-can-learn-from-women.

22. Avivah Wittenberg-Cox, "What Do Countries with the Best Coronavirus Responses Have in Common? Women Leaders," *Forbes*, April 2020, https://www.forbes.com/sites/avivahwittenbergcox/2020/04/13/what-do-countries-with-the-best-coronavirus-reponses-have-in-common-women-leaders/#44ea2e33dec4.

23. Robert B. Kaiser and Robert E. Kaplan, "Thatcher's Greatest Strength Was Her Greatest Weakness," *Harvard Business Review*, April 16, 2013, https://hbr.org/2013/04/thatchers-greatest-strength-was.

24. Austen, *Emma*, ed. Cronin and McMillan, 408.

25. Wittenberg-Cox.

26. Michaela J. Kerrissey and Amy C. Edmondson, "What Good Leaderships Looks Like during This Pandemic," *Harvard Business Review*, April 13, 2020, https://hbr.org/2020/04/what-good-leadership-looks-like-during-this-pandemic.

27. Brené Brown, *Dare to Lead: Brave Work, Tough Conversations, Whole Hearts* (New York: Penguin Random House, 2018), iBook edition, 72–73.

28. Belinda Luscombe, "A Year after Christchurch, Jacinda Ardern Has the World's Attention: How Will She Use It?" *Time*, March 2–March 9, 2020, https://time.com/magazine/south-pacific/5787631/march-3rd-2020-vol-195-no-7-asia-europe-middle-east-and-africa-south-america-south-pacific/.

29. Austen, *Emma*, ed. Cronin and McMillan, 407–8.

30. Austen, 409.

31. Tave, 246–47.

32. Anderson, 170.

33. Sr. Frances Ryan, in discussion with the author, March 3, 2018.

34. Austen, *Emma*, ed. Cronin and McMillan, 409.

35. Carol Dweck, *Mindset: The New Psychology of Success* (New York: Random House, 2016), 18.

36. Dweck, 18–19.

37. Dweck, 19.

38. Dweck, 20.

39. Helen Baxendale, "Backlash and Beyond: What Lies Ahead for Teach for America," *Education Week*, May 29, 2020, https://blogs.edweek .org/edweek/rick_hess_straight_up/2020/05/backlash_and_beyond _what_lies_ahead_for_teach_for_america.html.

40. Covey, 233.

41. Leah, in discussion with the author, September 29, 2018.

42. Sharon, in discussion with the author, October 23, 2018.

43. Robin DiAngelo, *White Fragility: Why It's So Hard for White People to Talk about Racism* (Boston: Beacon Press, 2018), 14.

Chapter 7.
Putting It All Together

1. Ralph Waldo Emerson, "Self-Reliance," in *Selections from Ralph Waldo Emerson*, ed. Stephen E. Whicher (Boston: Houghton Mifflin, 1957), 151.

Bibliography

Anderson, Kathleen. *Jane Austen's Women: An Introduction*. Albany: State University of New York Press, 2018.

Auerbach, Emily. *Searching for Jane Austen*. Madison: University of Wisconsin Press, 2004.

Austen, Jane. *The Annotated Emma*. Annotated and edited by David M. Shapard. New York: Anchor Books, 2012.

———. *The Annotated Mansfield Park*. Annotated and edited by David M. Shapard. New York: Anchor Books, 2017.

———. *The Annotated Persuasion*. Annotated and edited by David M. Shapard. New York: Anchor Books, 2010.

———. *The Annotated Pride and Prejudice*. Annotated and edited by David M. Shapard. New York: Anchor Books, 2012.

———. *The Annotated Sense and Sensibility*. Annotated and edited by David M. Shapard. New York: Anchor Books, 2011.

———. *Emma*. Edited by Richard Cronin and Dorothy McMillan. Cambridge: Cambridge University Press, 2013.

———. *Emma: An Annotated Edition*. Edited by Bharat Tandon. Cambridge: Belknap Press of Harvard University Press, 2012.

———. *Mansfield Park*. Edited by John Wiltshire. Cambridge: Cambridge University Press, 2013.

———. *Northanger Abbey*. Edited by Barbara M. Benedict and Dierdre Le Faye. Cambridge: Cambridge University Press, 2013.

———. *Persuasion*. Edited by Janet Todd and Antje Blank. Cambridge: Cambridge University Press, 2013.

———. *Persuasion: An Annotated Edition*. Edited by Robert Morrison. Cambridge: Belknap Press of Harvard University Press, 2011.

———. *Pride and Prejudice*. Edited by Pat Rogers. Cambridge: Cambridge University Press, 2013.

———. *Pride and Prejudice*. New York: Harper Perennial, 2018.

———. *Pride and Prejudice: An Annotated Edition*. Edited by Patricia Meyer Spacks. Cambridge: Belknap Press of Harvard University Press, 2010.

———. *Sense and Sensibility.* Edited by Edward Copeland. Cambridge: Cambridge University Press, 2013.

———. *Sense and Sensibility.* Edited by Patricia Meyer Spacks. Cambridge: Belknap Press of Harvard University Press, 2013.

Baxendale, Helen. "Backlash and Beyond: What Lies Ahead for Teach for America." *Education Week*, May 29, 2020, https://blogs.edweek.org /edweek/rick_hess_straight_up/2020/05/backlash_and_beyond_what _lies_ahead_for_teach_for_america.html.

Beard, Alison. "Mindfulness in the Age of Complexity: An Interview with Ellen Langer." Chap. 1 in *Mindfulness*. HBR Emotional Intelligence Series. Boston: Harvard Business School Publishing, 2017.

Berinato, Scott. "That Discomfort You're Feeling Is Grief." *Harvard Business Review*, March 2020. https://hbr.org/2020/03/that-discomfort -youre-feeling-is-grief.

Boyle, Brendan. "6 Ways to Integrate Play into the Workplace," *Inc.*, July 2015. https://www.inc.com/brendan-boyle/play-has-a-pr-problem.html.

Brickman, Philip, Dan Coates, and Ronnie Janoff-Bulman. "Lottery Winners and Accident Victims: Is Happiness Relative?" *Journal of Personality and Social Psychology* 36, no. 8 (1978). https://doi.org/10.1037 /0022-3514.36.8.917.

Brown, Brené. *Dare to Lead: Brave Work, Tough Conversations, Whole Hearts*. New York: Random House, 2018.

Brown, Tim. *Change by Design: How Design Thinking Transforms Organizations and Inspires Innovation*. New York: HarperCollins, 2009.

Brown, Tina. "What Happens When Women Stop Leading Like Men: Jacinda Ardern, Nancy Pelosi and the Power of Female Grace." *New York Times*, March 30, 2019. https://www.nytimes.com/2019/03/30 /opinion/women-leadership-jacinda-ardern.html.

Brownstein, Rachel M. *Why Jane Austen?* New York: Columbia University Press, 2011.

Brzezinski, Mika. *Know Your Value: Women, Money, and Getting What You're Worth*. Rev. ed. New York: Hachette Books, 2018.

Chamorro-Premuzic, Tomas, and Cindy Gallop. "7 Leadership Lessons Men Can Learn from Women." *Harvard Business Review*, April 1, 2020. https://hbr.org/2020/04/7-leadership-lessons-men-can-learn-from -women.

Chopra, Deepak. *The Seven Spiritual Laws of Success*. San Rafael: Amber-Allen, 1995.

"Christine Blasey Ford's Opening Statement for Senate Hearing." NPR, September 26, 2018. https://www.npr.org/2018/09/26/651941113/read-christine-blasey-fords-opening-statement-for-senate-hearing.

Chuter, Sharon. "How I Built Resilience: Live with Sharon Chuter." How I Built This with Guy Raz, July 9, 2020. https://www.npr.org/2020/07/08/889030664/how-i-built-resilience-live-with-sharon-chuter.

Collins, Jim. "Level 5 Leadership: The Triumph of Humility and Fierce Resolve." Harvard Business Review, January 2001. https://hbr.org/2001/01/level-5-leadership-the-triumph-of-humility-and-fierce-resolve-2.

Conrad, Peter. Introduction to Pride and Prejudice, by Jane Austen, ix–xxix. New York: Everyman's Library, 1991.

Corliss, Julie. "Six Relaxation Techniques to Reduce Stress." Harvard Health Publishing, September 2016, updated September 10, 2019. https://www.health.harvard.edu/mind-and-mood/six-relaxation-techniques-to-reduce-stress.

Coutu, Diane L. "How Resilience Works." Harvard Business Review, May 2002. Reprinted in HBR's 10 Must Reads Collection. Boston: Harvard Business Review Press, 2014. https://hbr.org/2002/05/how-resilience-works.

Covey, Stephen R. The Seven Habits of Highly Effective People. Coral Gables: Mango, 2016.

Csikszentmihalyi, Mihaly. Flow. New York: HarperCollins e-books, 1990. Apple Books.

Dadlez, E. M. Jane Austen's "Emma": Philosophical Perspectives. New York: Oxford University Press, 2018.

Dalio, Ray. Principles. New York: Simon and Schuster, 2017.

Denning, Steve. "The Best of Peter Drucker." Forbes, June 2014. https://www.forbes.com/sites/stevedenning/2014/07/29/the-best-of-peter-drucker/#3f1ad2e95a96.

Dethmer, Jim, Diana Chapman, and Kaley Warner Klemp. The 15 Commitments of Conscious Leadership: A New Paradigm for Sustainable Success. United States: Conscious Leadership Group, 2015.

DiAngelo, Robin. White Fragility: Why It's So Hard for White People to Talk about Racism. Boston: Beacon Press, 2018.

Drucker, Peter. Managing Oneself. Boston: Harvard Business Review Press, 2010.

Dweck, Carol. Mindset: The New Psychology of Success. New York: Random House, 2016.

Eagly, Alice, and Linda Lorene Carli. *Through the Labyrinth: The Truth about How Women Become Leaders*. Boston: Harvard Business School Press, 2007.

Eldridge, Richard. "'A Danger at Present Unperceived': Self-Understanding, Imagination, Emotion, and Social Stance in *Emma*." In *Jane Austen's "Emma": Philosophical Perspectives,* edited by E. M. Dadlez. Oxford: Oxford University Press, 2018.

Emerson, Ralph Waldo. "Self-Reliance." In *Selections from Ralph Waldo Emerson*, edited by Stephen E. Whicher. Boston: Houghton Mifflin, 1957.

Epley, Nicholas, and Amit Kumar. "How to Design an Ethical Organization: A Behavioral Approach." *Harvard Business Review*, May-June 2019. https://hbr.org/2019/05/how-to-design-an-ethical-organization.

Fisher, Roger, William Ury, and Bruce Patton. *Getting to Yes: Negotiating Agreement without Giving In*. London: Penguin Group, 1991.

Frankl, Viktor. *Man's Search for Meaning*. Boston: Beacon Press, 2006.

Fryer, Bronwyn, and Howard Gardner. "The Ethical Mind." *Harvard Business Review*, March 2007. https://hbr.org/2007/03/the-ethical-mind.

Garner, Bethany. "Female Leadership during COVID-19: What Can We Learn?" *BusinessBecause*, June 19, 2020. https://www.businessbecause.com/news/insights/7028/learn-female-leadership-covid-19.

Gentile, Mary C. *Giving Voice to Values: How to Speak Your Mind When You Know What's Right*. New Haven: Yale University Press, 2010.

George, Bill, Peter Sims, Andrew N. McLean, and Diana Mayer. "Discovering Your Authentic Leadership." *Harvard Business Review*, February 2007. https://hbr.org/2007/02/discovering-your-authentic-leadership.

Gilligan, Carol. *In a Different Voice: Psychological Theory and Women's Development*. Cambridge: Harvard University Press, 1982, 1993.

Goleman, Daniel. *Daniel Goleman* (blog). http://www.danielgoleman.info/women-leaders-get-results-the-data/.

———. "The Focused Leader." In *Focus: HBR Emotional Intelligence Series*. Boston: Harvard Business Review, 2018.

Goleman, Daniel, Richard Boyatzis, and Annie McKee. *Primal Leadership: Unleashing the Power of Emotional Intelligence*. With a new preface by the authors. Boston: Harvard Business Review Press, 2013.

Graham-McLay, Charlotte. "New Zealand Passes Law Banning Most Semi-automatic Weapons, Weeks after Massacre." *New York Times*, April 10, 2019. https://www.nytimes.com/2019/04/10/world/asia/new-zealand-guns-jacinda-ardern.html.

Greenleaf, Robert K. "What Is Servant Leadership?" https://www.green
leaf.org/what-is-servant-leadership/.

Heifetz, Ronald A., and Marty Linsky. "A Survival Guide for Leaders."
In *HBR's 10 Must Reads on Change Management*. Boston: Harvard
Business Review.

Hogan, Kevin. "Five Ways Ruth Bader Ginsburg Made a Difference, Stayed
Connected to Cornell." *Ithaca Journal*, September 19, 2020, updated
September 21, 2020. https://www.ithacajournal.com/story/news/local
/2020/09/19/rbg-supreme-court-ruth-bader-ginsburg-graduate-cornell
-1954-five-ways-made-difference/5841271002/.

Iger, Robert Allen. *The Ride of a Lifetime: Lessons Learned from 15 Years
as CEO of the Walt Disney Company*. New York: Random House, 2019.
Apple Books.

James, Aaron. *Assholes: A Theory of Donald Trump*. New York: Doubleday,
2016. Apple Books.

Jonker, Julian, and Shaun Harper. "The College Cheating Scandal: The
Biggest Victim Is Public Confidence." *Knowledge at Wharton*, March
2019. https://knowledge.wharton.upenn.edu/article/college-admissions
-scandal/#comments.

Kaiser, Robert B., and Robert E. Kaplan. "Thatcher's Greatest Strength
Was Her Greatest Weakness." *Harvard Business Review*, April 2013.
https://hbr.org/2013/04/thatchers-greatest-strength-was.

Kayne Kaufman, Andrea. "You're Fired! Donald Trump, No Child Left
Behind, and the Limits of Dissonant Leadership in Education." *Journal
of Women in Educational Leadership* (2005): 193–212.

Kelly, Helena. *Jane Austen, the Secret Radical*. New York: Vintage Books,
2016.

Kerrissey, Michaela J., and Amy C. Edmondson. "What Good Leadership Looks Like during This Pandemic." *Harvard Business Review*,
April 13, 2020. https://hbr.org/2020/04/what-good-leadership-looks
-like-during-this-pandemic.

King, Michelle. "Leaders, Stop Denying the Gender Inequity in Your
Organization." *Harvard Business Review*, June 18, 2020.

Kübler-Ross, Elisabeth, and David Kessler. *On Grief and Grieving: Finding
the Meaning of Grief through the Five Stages of Loss*. New York: Simon
and Schuster, 2005.

Liu, Alex. "Making Joy a Priority at Work." *Harvard Business Review*,
July 2019.

Liu, Jennifer. "This Harvard MBA Grad Worked at a Starbucks after

Graduation—Then She Founded a Company Worth Millions." CNBC, last modified January 13, 2020. https://www.cnbc.com/2020/01/10 /tatchas-vicky-tsai-worked-at-starbucks-after-harvard-business-school .html.

Looser, Devoney. *The Making of Jane Austen*. Baltimore: Johns Hopkins University Press, 2017.

Luetkenhaus, Holly, and Zoe Weinstein. *Austentatious: The Evolving World of Jane Austen Fans*. Iowa City: University of Iowa Press, 2019.

Luscombe, Belinda. "A Year after Christchurch, Jacinda Ardern Has the World's Attention, How Will She Use It?" *Time Magazine*, February 2020. https://time.com/5787443/jacinda-ardern-christchurch-new -zealand-anniversary/.

Margolis, Joshua D., and Paul G. Stolz. "How to Bounce Back from Adversity." In *HBR's 10 Must Reads on Mental Toughness*, 77–88. Boston: Harvard Business Review Press, 2018.

Menendez, Alicia. *The Likeability Trap: How to Break Free and Succeed as You Are*. New York: Harper Business, 2019.

Mitchell, Stephen. *Tao Te Ching: A New English Version*. New York: HarperCollins e-books, 1994.

———. *Tao Te Ching*. New York: Harper Books, 1999.

Morin, Rebecca, Sarah Elbeshbishi, and Caren Bohan. "'We Can All Relate to This': Why AOC's Speech on Sexism Struck a Chord beyond Washington." *USA Today*, July 25, 2020. https://www.usatoday.com /story/news/politics/2020/07/25/aoc-speech-rebuking-ted-yoho-struck -chord-well-beyond-washington/5506707002/.

Morris, Ivor. *Mr. Collins Considered: Approaches to Jane Austen*. New York: Routledge and Kegan, 1987.

Morse, Gardiner. "The Science behind the Smile: An Interview with Daniel Gilbert by Gardiner Morse." In *Emotional Intelligence: Happiness*. Boston: Harvard Business Review Press, 2017.

Nhat Hanh, Thich. *How to Fight*. Berkeley: Parallax Press, 2017.

Osterweil, Scot. "The 4 Freedoms of Play & Learning." Playful Learning, April 25, 2007. http://playfullearning.com/4freedoms/.

Pollan, Stephen M., and Mark Levine. *Fire Your Boss*. New York: Harper-Collins, 2004.

Prime, Jeanine L., Nancy M. Carter, and Theresa M. Welbourne. "Women 'Take Care,' Men 'Take Charge': Managers' Stereotypic Perceptions of Women and Men Leaders." *Psychologist-Manager Journal* 12, no. 1 (2009): 25–49. doi:10.1080/10887150802371799.

Raz, Guy. "Cisco Systems & Urban Decay: Sandy Lerner." *How I Built This with Guy Raz*. Podcast audio, October 1, 2018. https://www.npr .org/2018/09/28/652663380/cisco-systems-urban-decay-sandy-lerner.

Reardon, Kathleen. "The Memo Every Woman Keeps in Her Desk." In *HBR's 10 Must Reads on Women and Leadership*. Boston: Harvard Business Review Press, 2019. https://hbr.org/1993/03/the-memo-every -woman-keeps-in-her-desk.

Russaw, Jeanine Marie. "8 Ruth Bader Ginsburg Quotes That Define the Supreme Court Justice's Legacy." *Newsweek*, September 18, 2020. https://www.newsweek.com/8-ruth-bader-ginsburg-quotes-that-define -supreme-court-justices-legacy-1471585.

Schulte, Brigid. *Overwhelmed: Work, Love, and Play When No One Has the Time*. New York: Farrar, Straus and Giroux e-books, 2014. Apple Books.

Schwartz, Tony, and Catherine McCarthy. "Manage Your Energy, Not Your Time." *Harvard Business Review*, October 2007.

Shacknai, Gabby. "Uoma Beauty's Sharon Chuter Is Holding Brands Accountable with 'Pull Up or Shut Up.'" *Forbes*, June 8, 2020, https:// www.forbes.com/sites/gabbyshacknai/2020/06/08/uoma-beautys -sharon-chuter-is-holding-brands-accountable-with-pull-up-or-shut-up /#38b33b9370de.

Sinek, Simon. *Leaders Eat Last*. New York: Penguin Random House, 2014. Apple Books.

Smith, David G., Judith E. Rosenstein, and Margaret C. Nikolov. "The Different Words We Use to Describe Male and Female Leaders." *Harvard Business Review*, May 25, 2018. https://hbr.org/2018/05/the -different-words-we-use-to-describe-male-and-female-leaders.

"Stress Management: Relaxing Your Mind and Body." Michigan Medicine. Last modified June 28, 2018. https://www.uofmhealth.org/health -library/uz2209.

Tannen, Deborah. "The Power of Talk: Who Gets Heard and Why." *Harvard Business Review*, September-October 1995. https://hbr.org/1995/09 /the-power-of-talk-who-gets-heard-and-why.

Tave, Stuart M. *Some Words of Jane Austen*. Chicago: University of Chicago Press, 2019.

Thoreau, Henry David. *Walden, Or, Life in the Woods*. United Kingdom: Delphi Classics, 2013. IBook edition.

Thunberg, Greta. "You're Acting like Spoiled Irresponsible Children." European Economic and Social Committee, February 21, 2019. https://

www.eesc.europa.eu/en/news-media/videos/youre-acting-spoiled
-irresponsible-children-speech-greta-thunberg-climate-activist.

Trilling, Lionel. *The Moral Obligation to Be Intelligent: Selected Essays.*
Edited by Leon Wieseltier. New York: Farrar, Straus and Giroux e-book,
2000.

Tsui, Bonnie. "You Are Doing Something Important When You Aren't
Doing Anything: We Need to Rest, to Read, to Reconnect." *New York
Times*, June 21, 2019. https://www.nytimes.com/2019/06/21/opinion
/summer-lying-fallow.html.

Twenge, Jean M., and W. Keith Campbell. *The Narcissism Epidemic: Living
in the Age of Entitlement.* New York: Atria Books, 2009. Apple Books.

Ury, William. *Getting to Yes with Yourself: And Other Worthy Opponents.*
New York: HarperCollins Publishers, 2015.

Wall, Celia J., and Pat Gannon-Leary. "A Sentence Made by Men: Muted
Group Theory Revisited." *European Journal of Women's Studies* 6, no. 1
(1999), https://journals.sagepub.com/doi/abs/10.1177/1350506899006
00103.

Wittenberg-Cox, Avivah. "What Do Countries with the Best Coronavirus
Responses Have in Common? Women Leaders." *Forbes*, April 13, 2020.
https://www.forbes.com/sites/avivahwittenbergcox/2020/04/13/what
-do-countries-with-the-best-coronavirus-reponses-have-in-common
-women-leaders/#44ea2e33dec4.

Young-Eisendrath, Polly. *The Self-Esteem Trap: Raising Confident and
Compassionate Kids in an Age of Self-Importance.* New York: Little,
Brown, 2008. Apple Books.

Zander, Benjamin, and Rosamund Stone Zander. *The Art of Possibility.*
New York: Penguin Publishing Group, 2000. IBooks.

Index